Stitch Workshop

Right-Angle Weave

basic techniques, advanced results

KB
KALMBACH BOOKS

From the publisher of
Bead&Button magazine

Kalmbach Books
21027 Crossroads Circle
Waukesha, Wisconsin 53186
www.Kalmbach.com/Books

Published in 2011
16 15 14 13 12   2 3 4 5 6

Manufactured in the United States of America

ISBN: 978-0-87116-455-1

The material in this book has appeared previously in
Bead&Button magazine and the *Bead&Button* special
issue *Beading Basics: Right-Angle Weave*. *Bead&Button*
is registered as a trademark.

Compiled and edited by: Elisa Neckar
Art Direction: Lisa Bergman
Layout: Rebecca Markstein
Illustration: Kellie Jaeger
Photography: Bill Zuback, Jim Forbes

Publisher's Cataloging-In-Publication Data

Right-angle weave : basic techniques, advanced results / [from
the publisher of Bead&Button magazine].

   p. : ill. (some col.) ; cm. – (Stitch workshop ; 2)

   "The material in this book has appeared previously in
Bead&Button magazine and the Bead&Button special issue
Beading Basics: Right-Angle Weave."–T.p. verso.

   ISBN: 978-0-87116-455-1

   1. Beadwork–Patterns. 2. Beadwork–Handbooks, manuals,
etc. 3. Jewelry making–Handbooks, manuals, etc. I. Kalmbach
Publishing Company. II. Title: Bead&Button magazine. III.
Title: Beading basics : right-angle weave.

TT860 .R54 2011
745.594/2

Contents

Right-Angle Weave and Stitching Basics

Projects

Introduction

Right-angle weave's not just about rectangular designs. In fact, variety's the name of the game when it comes to the right-angle weave projects included in this second volume of the *Stitch Workshop* series.

First, there's a variety of skill levels represented in this book. Using the simple techniques explored in the "Right-Angle Weave Basics" section (p. 5), you'll find yourself working through 28 projects — organized by difficulty level — that explore this popular stitch, from the simplest right-angle weave designs through more complex tubular, cubic, and spiral versions of the stitch.

That variety can also be used to create nearly any jewelry piece, including necklaces, bracelets, and earrings, in any style. Try your hand at bangles like Shelly Nybakke's in "What's Your Bangle" (p. 56) or saucer earrings, like Deborah Staehle's in "Cosmic Crystals" (p. 28). The projects utilize a multitude of materials — right-angle weave isn't limited to seed beads! It can be worked in crystals, pearls, and fire-polished glass beads, for wide range of stunning looks.

And the finished products featured, though all created in the same stitch, will astonish you with their differences. Check out the curves of Lesley Weiss's "Mandala Medallions" (p. 71) or try the open latticework of Abby Cobb's "Crystalline Bracelet" (p. 44) for just a small sampling of the eye-catching mix of designs.

Whether you're new to right-angle weave or an experienced beader, you'll love the variety — of all kinds — that right-angle weave offers you!

Right-Angle Weave Basics

Right-angle weave is an off-loom beadweaving technique in which the beads of each stitch form a small square. Each stitch forms a new square that shares a side with the previous square. In its most basic form, each side of the square is made up of one bead, though many projects use more than one bead per side. In right-angle weave, the beads sit at right angles to each other (thus the name of the stitch), and create a beautifully flexible, slightly airy fabric. Because you pick up several beads per stitch, it can work up quickly, especially when you use larger beads.

Beadwork made in right-angle weave is evident in several cultures. Some of the beadwork dates as far back as the 1600s. David Chatt's development and expansion of this technique beginning in the 1980s is largely responsible for the widespread interest in and use of right-angle weave today.

Flat right-angle weave

The following instructions are for basic right-angle weave using one bead per side. For projects that use more than one bead per side, the thread path is essentially the same as for the basic stitch; treat each set of beads on each side of the square as a single bead.

[1] To start the first row of right-angle weave, pick up four beads, and tie them into a ring. Sew through the first three beads again.

[2] Pick up three beads. Sew through the last bead of the previous ring **(a–b)**, and continue through the first two beads picked up in this stitch **(b–c)**.

[3] Continue adding three beads per stitch until the first row is the desired length, alternating direction with each stitch.

[4] To begin row 2, sew through the last stitch in row 1, exiting the end bead at the edge of one long side.

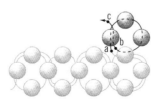

[5] Pick up three beads, and sew through the bead your thread exited in the previous step **(a–b)**. Continue through the first new bead **(b–c)**.

[6] Pick up two beads, and sew through the next top bead in the previous row and the bead your thread exited in the previous stitch **(a–b)**. Continue through the two new beads and the next top bead of the previous row **(b–c)**.

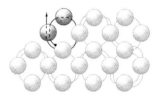

[7] Pick up two beads, and sew through the last two beads your thread went through in the previous stitch and the first new bead. Keep moving your thread in a circular motion, and pick up two beads per stitch for the rest of the row. Continue adding rows for the desired length.

Tubular right-angle weave

Right-angle weave can be worked in rounds to create narrow tubes or large cylindrical objects like purse or vase coverings.

[1] Work a flat strip of right-angle weave that is one stitch fewer than needed for the desired circumference of the tube.

[2] Connect the last stitch to the first stitch as follows: Exit the end bead of the last stitch, pick up a bead, and sew through the first bead of the first stitch. Pick up a bead and sew through the end bead of the last stitch. Exit as shown above.

[3] To begin the next round, sew through to exit a bead along the top edge. Pick up three beads, and sew

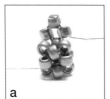 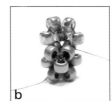 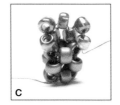 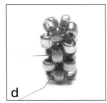

through the bead your thread just exited and the three new beads **(photo a)**. Sew through the next top bead in the previous round.

[4] Pick up two beads, and sew through the side bead in the previous stitch, the top bead, the top bead your thread exited at the start of this step **(photo b)**, and the side bead in the new stitch.

[5] Pick up two beads, and sew through the next top bead in the previous round, the side bead your thread exited at the start of this step, the two new beads **(photo c)**, and the next top bead in the previous round.

[6] If your tube is more than four stitches around, repeat steps 4 and 5 until there is one uncompleted stitch in the round.

[7] Depending upon how many stitches there are in each round, your thread will either be exiting a top bead in the previous round or the side bead in the last stitch added in this round. If the latter, you're ready to work the final stitch of the round. If the former, sew up through the side bead in the first stitch of this round. Pick up a bead, and sew through the other unconnected side bead in this round **(photo d)**. Sew through the final stitch, exiting the new top bead added in this stitch.

[8] Repeat steps 3–7 for the desired length.

Cubic right-angle weave

Cubic right-angle weave creates sturdy three-dimensional beadwork that makes beautiful, architectural jewelry. It can be worked as a single row of cubes for a rope with a square profile, or you can stitch additional rows for thick bands of beadwork.

[1] Pick up four beads, and tie them into a ring with a square knot (Basics, p. 8). Sew through the next two beads again.

[2] Pick up three beads, and sew through the bead your thread exited at the start of this step and the next bead in the original ring.

[3] Pick up two beads, and sew through the adjacent bead in the previous stitch, the bead your thread just exited in the original ring, and the next bead in the ring.

[4] Repeat step 3, and continue through the adjacent bead in the stitch added in step 2.

[5] Pick up a bead, and sew through the adjacent bead from the previous stitch, the bead in the original ring, and the first two beads in the stitch added in step 2.

[6] Sew through the top bead in the next three stitches and the bead your thread exited at the start of this step.

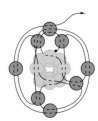

[7] Repeat steps 2–6 for the desired length.

TIPS AND TRICKS FOR RIGHT-ANGLE WEAVE

David Chatt's development of the single-needle right-angle weave was a driving force behind the popularization of right-angle weave today. David enjoys sharing his tips and tricks for the technique with people making the same discoveries that he did. Here are 10 tips that will help you learn flat right-angle weave.

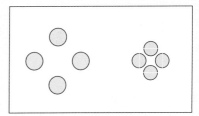

FIGURES 1A AND 1B

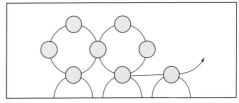

FIGURE 2

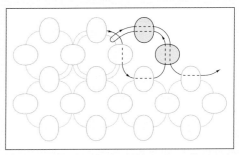

FIGURE 3

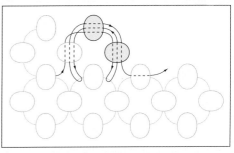

FIGURE 4

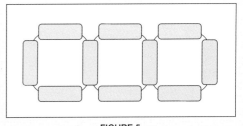

FIGURE 5

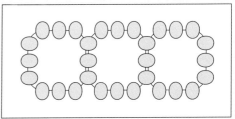

FIGURE 6

1 Think of each four-bead unit as a square with a north, south, east, and west bead. The east bead from the previous square becomes the west bead for the next. The north beads from the previous row are the south beads for the new row. Try to keep this grid system in mind as you work. You can use graph paper to work out designs, with each square representing a bead or each line segment representing a bead (**figures 1a and 1b**).

2 Follow your thread. This will help you determine how to position your thread before beginning the next stitch.

3 Always turn a corner into the next bead, unless you are varying the stitch by increasing or decreasing. The beads may appear to be lined up, but if you can imagine them as part of a grid system occupying a side of a square unit, this tip will help you to understand the underlying logic of right-angle weave.

4 Never cross an intersection or go directly from one bead into the next, unless you are increasing or decreasing. Remember, it is called "right-angle" weave. Don't be tempted to cross the intersection as shown in **figure 2**. Turn the corner!

5 Each stitch can usually be made in two motions. In the first motion make the unit. In the second motion, position the thread so that you are ready to pick up beads for the next unit.

Develop this habit early on, and you won't fall into the trap of thinking that sewing through one bead at a time is a more careful approach. That only allows for opportunities to make mistakes.

6 Use beads with good open centers. You have to pass through each bead a number of times, so having good open-mouthed beads will help you to avoid "Oh *%#@!" moments.

7 If there is too much thread in a bead to allow for an additional pass-through of your needle, loop the thread around the thread that formed the previous unit and reverse direction. I call this technique "cheat-a-bead." It is perhaps the best innovation I have ever come up with (**figures 3 and 4**).

8 Practice with oval beads or multiple beads per side (**figures 5 and 6**). This makes the square formed by each unit easier to identify.

9 When learning, use two contrasting colors of beads, switching back and forth between them for each row. You may also use another color for the thread. Black and white beads with red thread is a perfect combo. Make sure that your beads are the same size.

10 Have fun, experiment, and don't look for instant gratification. This work is best thought of as a meditation rather than a meal ticket.

Beading Technique Basics

THREAD AND KNOTS

Adding thread
To add a thread, sew into the beadwork several rows prior to the point where the last bead was added. Sew through the beadwork, following the thread path of the stitch. Tie a few half-hitch knots (see **Half-hitch knot**) between beads, and exit where the last stitch ended.

Conditioning thread
Use either beeswax or microcrystalline wax (not candle wax or paraffin) or Thread Heaven to condition nylon thread. Wax smooths the nylon fibers and adds tackiness that will stiffen your beadwork slightly. Thread Heaven adds a static charge that causes the thread to repel itself, so don't use it with doubled thread. Stretch the thread, then pull it through the conditioner.

Ending thread
To end a thread, sew back into the beadwork, following the existing thread path and tying two or three half-hitch knots (see **Half-hitch knot**) between beads as you go. Change directions as you sew so the thread crosses itself. Sew through a few beads after the last knot, and trim the thread.

Half-hitch knot
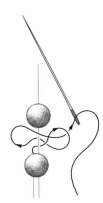
Pass the needle under the thread between two beads. A loop will form as you pull the thread through. Cross back over the thread between the beads, sew through the loop, and pull gently to draw the knot into the beadwork.

Square knot

[1] Cross the left-hand end of the thread over the right, and bring it under and back up.

[2] Cross the end that is now on the right over the left, go through the loop, and pull both ends to tighten.

Surgeon's knot
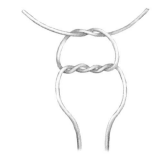

[1] Cross the left-hand end of the thread over the right twice. Pull to tighten.
[2] Cross the end that is now on the right over the left, go through the loop, and tighten.

Stop bead

Use a stop bead to secure beads temporarily when you begin stitching. Choose a bead that is distinctly different from the beads in your project. String the stop bead, and sew through it again in the same

direction. If desired, sew through it one more time for added security.

Ladder stitch
Traditional method
[1] Pick up two beads, sew through the first bead again, and then sew through the second bead **(a–b)**.

[2] Add subsequent beads by picking up one bead, sewing through the previous bead, and then sewing through the new bead **(b–c)**. Continue for the desired length.

This technique produces uneven tension, which you can easily correct by zigzagging back through the beads in the opposite direction.

Alternative method

[1] Pick up all the beads you need to reach the length your pattern requires. Fold the last two beads so they are parallel, and sew through the second-to-last bead again in the same direction **(a–b)**.

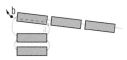

[2] Fold the next loose bead so it sits parallel to the previous bead in the ladder, and sew through the loose bead

Tools & Materials

Excellent tools and materials for making jewelry are available in bead and craft stores, through catalogs, and on the Internet. Here are the essential supplies you'll need for the projects in this book.

Tools

Chainnose pliers have smooth, flat inner jaws, and the tips taper to a point. Use them for gripping and for opening and closing loops and jump rings.

Roundnose pliers have smooth, tapered, conical jaws used to make loops. The closer to the tip you work, the smaller the loop will be.

Use the front of a **wire cutters'** blades to make a pointed cut and the back of the blades to make a flat cut. Do not use your jewelry-grade wire cutters on memory wire, which is extremely hard; use heavy-duty wire cutters or bend the memory wire back and forth until it breaks.

Crimping pliers have two grooves in their jaws that are used to fold or roll a crimp bead into a compact shape.

Beading needles are coded by size. The higher the number, the finer the beading needle. Unlike sewing needles, the eye of a beading needle is almost as narrow as its shaft. In addition to the size of the bead, the number of times you will pass through the bead also affects the needle size that you will use; if you will pass through a bead multiple times, you need to use a smaller needle.

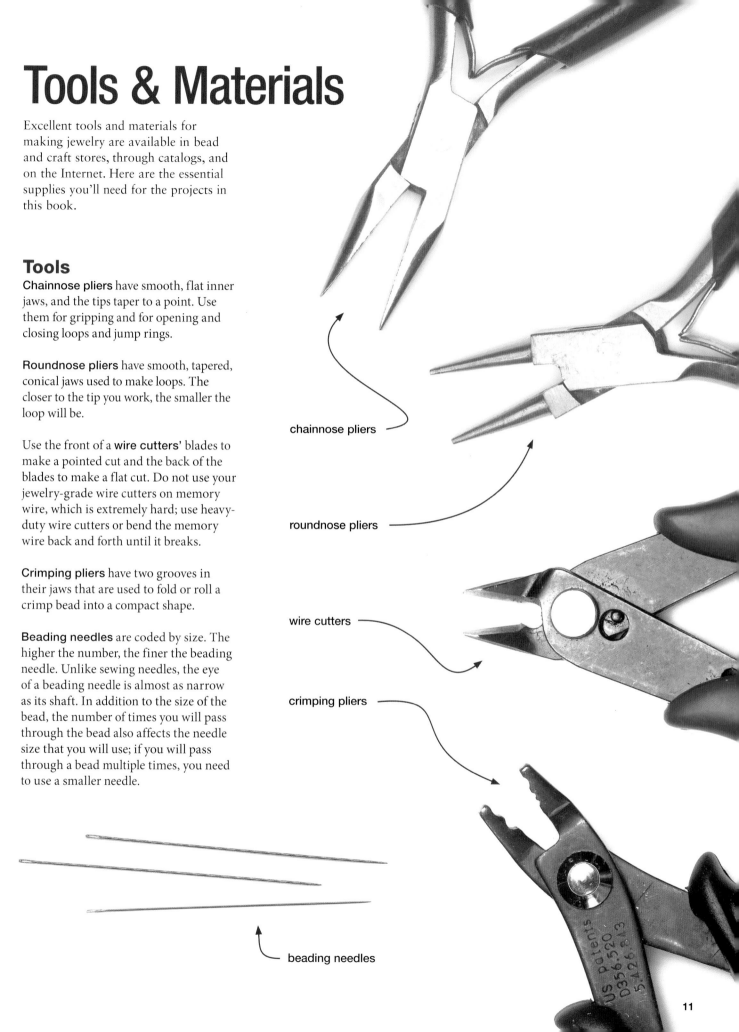

chainnose pliers

roundnose pliers

wire cutters

crimping pliers

beading needles

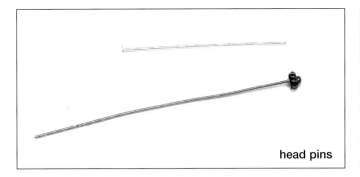

head pins

jump rings

Findings

A **head pin** looks like a long, blunt, thick sewing pin. It has a flat or decorative head on one end to keep beads on. Head pins come in different metals, diameters (or gauges), and lengths.

A **jump ring** is used to connect two loops. It is a small wire circle, oval, or decorative shape that is either soldered closed or comes with a split so you can twist the jump ring open and closed.

Crimp beads are large-hole, thin-walled metal beads designed to be flattened or crimped into a tight roll. Use them when stringing jewelry on flexible beading wire. **Crimp bead covers** provide a way to hide your crimps by covering them with a finding that mimics the look of a small bead.

Earring findings come in a huge variety of metals and styles, including post, French hook, hoop, and leverback. You will almost always want a loop (or loops) on earring findings so you can attach beads or beadwork.

Clasps come in many sizes and shapes. Some of the most common are the toggle, consisting of a ring and a bar; lobster claw, which opens when you pull on a tiny lever; S-hook and hook-and-eye, which link two soldered jump rings or split rings; slide, consisting of one tube that slides inside another; snap, consisting of a ball that inserts into a socket; and box, with a tab and a slot.

Bead caps are used to decorate one or both sides of a bead or gemstone.

Spacers are small beads used between larger beads to space the placement of the beads.

crimp beads

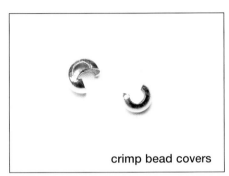

crimp bead covers

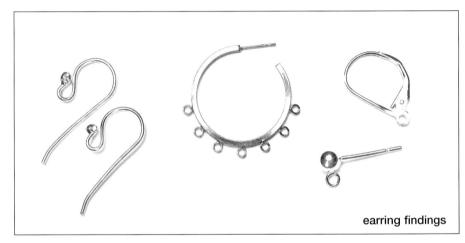

earring findings

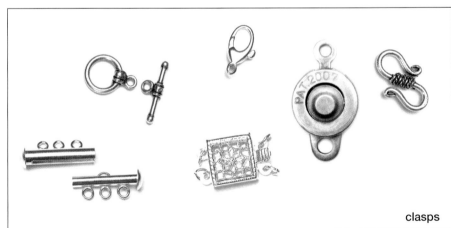

clasps

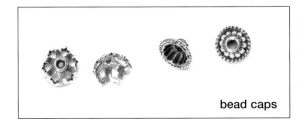

bead caps

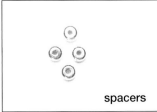

spacers

Stitching & stringing materials

Thread comes in many sizes and strengths. Size (diameter or thickness) is designated by a letter or number. OO, O, and A are the thinnest threads; B, D, E, F, and FF are subsequently thicker.

Plied gel-spun polyethylene (GSP), such as Power Pro or DandyLine, is made from polyethylene fibers that have been spun into two or more threads that are braided together. It is almost unbreakable, doesn't stretch, and resists fraying. The thickness can make it difficult to make multiple passes through a bead. It is ideal for stitching with larger beads, such as pressed glass and crystals. **Parallel filament GSP**, such as Fireline, is a single-ply thread made from spun and bonded polyethylene fibers. Because it's thin and strong, it's best for stitching with small seed beads.

flexible beading wire

Flexible beading wire is composed of steel wires twisted together and covered with nylon. This wire is much stronger than thread and does not stretch; the higher the number of inner strands (between three and 49), the more flexible and kink-resistant the wire. It is available in a variety of sizes and colors. Use .014 and .015 for most gemstones, crystals, and glass beads. Use thicker varieties, .018, .019, and .024, for heavy beads or nuggets. Use thinner wire, .010 and .012, for lightweight pieces and beads with very small holes, such as pearls.

Other threads are available, including **parallel filament nylon**, such as Nymo or C-Lon (best used in bead weaving and bead embroidery); **plied nylon thread**, such as Silamide (good for twisted fringe, bead crochet, and beadwork that needs a lot of body); and **polyester thread**, such as Gutermann (best for bead crochet or bead embroidery when the thread must match the fabric).

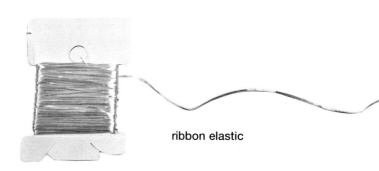

ribbon elastic

threads

Ribbon elastic such as Gossamer Floss is usually used for stretchy, slip-on bracelets with no clasp or closure that must expand to fit over the wearer's hand.

Beads

Many of the projects in this book will call for **seed beads** as the main elements of the design. The most common and highest quality seed beads are manufactured in Japan or the Czech Republic. These seed beads are the most uniform and predictable in size, shape, and hole size. Bead sizes are written as a number with a symbol, such as 11/0 or 11º (pronounced "eleven aught"). Sizes range from 2º (6mm) to 24º (smaller than 1mm) — the higher the number, the smaller the bead. The most common seed bead size is 11º, but most suppliers carry sizes ranging from 6º to 15º. Seed beads smaller than 15º are difficult to work with as their holes are tiny, and thus are rarely used and very hard to find.

Japanese cylinder beads, which are sold under the brand names Delicas, Treasures, or Aikos, are very consistent in shape and size. Unlike the standard round seed bead, they're shaped like little tubes and have very large, round holes and straight sides. They create an even surface texture when stitched together in beadwork. These beads are also sold in tubes or packages by weight. In addition to round and cylinder beads, there are several other seed bead shapes: **Hex-cut beads** are similar to cylinder beads, but instead of a smooth, round exterior, they have six sides. **Triangle beads** have three sides, and **cube beads** have four. **Bugle beads** are long, thin tubes that can range in size from 2 to 30mm long. You might also find tiny teardrop-shaped beads, called **drops** or **fringe drops**, and **magatamas**. Cube, drop, and bugle beads are sold by size, measured in millimeters (mm) rather than aught size.

Some projects may also use a variety of **accent beads** to embellish your stitched pieces, including **crystals**, **gemstones**, **fire-polished beads**, and **pearls**, to name only a few types.

The Cuff
Crystallized

The elegant shimmer of this cuff belies its simplicity

designed by **Pam O'Connor**

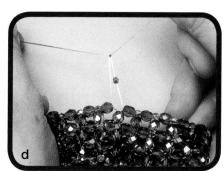

In less than two hours, you can whip up three rows of right-angle weave. Use aurora borealis fire-polished glass beads to achieve the aqueous gleam.

stepbystep

Bracelet

[1] Cut 2½ yd. (2.3m) of Gossamer Floss. String four 6mm fire-polished beads, alternating color A and color B. Leave a 2½-ft. (76cm) tail and tie the beads into a snug ring with a square knot (Basics, p. 8). Glue the knot and pull the knot into a bead.

[2] Thread a needle on the longer end and continue through a B, an A, and a B in the ring. Pick up an A, a B, and an A and sew through the B your thread exited in the ring. Continue through the next A and B in the new stitch.

[3] Pick up an A, a B, and an A, and sew through the B your thread just exited in the previous stitch. Repeat to add three-bead stitches until the chain almost reaches around your wrist with a ¼-in. (6mm) gap.

[4] Pick up an A and sew through the B at the other end of the chain. Pick up an A and sew through the last B in the chain to link the ends together **(photo a)**.

[5] To start the second round, sew through the next three beads of the connecting stitch, exiting an A. Pick up a B, an A, and a B and sew through the A your thread just exited **(photo b)**. Sew through the first B added in the new stitch.

[6] Pick up an A and a B, and sew through the next A in the first round **(photo c)**. Continue through the adjacent B in the previous stitch of round 2 and the two beads you just added.

[7] Sew through the next A in row 1. Pick up a B and an A. Sew through the B in the previous stitch, the round 1 A, and the B in the new stitch.

[8] Repeat steps 6 and 7 to complete the round. The last stitch needs only one A to join to the first stitch.

[9] Sew through the beads to the inside of the beadwork. Tie two half-hitch knots (Basics) close to a bead and glue the knot. Pull the knot into the bead. After the glue dries, stretch out the tail and cut it so that the end pulls back into the bead.

[10] Thread a needle on the long tail. Add a third round on the other side as in steps 5–9.

[11] Thread a needle on 12 in. (30cm) of Gossamer Floss. Sew through an A on the edge, leaving a 3-in. (7.6cm) tail. Pick up a color C 3mm fire-polished bead. Sew through the next edge A. Repeat around the entire edge. When you have strung the last 3mm, knot the ends snugly with a surgeon's knot (Basics and **photo d**) and glue the knot. Sew the thread tails through a bead on each side and pull the knot into a bead. After the glue dries, trim the tails. Repeat to add 3mms to the opposite edge.

MATERIALS LIST
bracelet 2½ in. (6.4cm) diameter
• **80** 6mm fire-polished beads, color A
• **60** 6mm fire-polished beads, color B
• **40** 3mm fire-polished beads, color C
• twisted wire beading needle
• Gossamer Floss or ribbon elastic
• G-S Hypo Cement

Crystal
Ribbon

Oblong metal beads join two strips of bicone crystals in different shades of the same hue

designed by **Nancy Zellers**

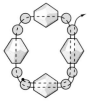

FIGURE 1

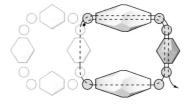

FIGURE 2

MATERIALS

bracelet 7 in. (18cm)

• **27** 7 x 5mm corrugated double-cone beads, gold-plated
• **71** 4mm bicone crystals in each of **2** colors*: A, B
• 1g 15º seed beads
• Fireline 6 lb. test
• beading needles, #10

* Bicone colors used in the bracelets shown are:
  blue bracelet: indicolite, Pacific opal
  purple bracelet: lilac, violet opal
  green bracelet: olivine, khaki

FIGURE 3

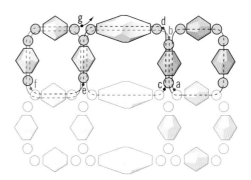

FIGURE 4

This bracelet works up quickly, and it is a great way to learn right-angle weave. It can display any color scheme — just choose two of your favorite crystal colors and pair them with metal accent beads.

stepbystep

Bracelet band

[1] On 4 yd. (3.7m) of Fireline, pick up a repeating pattern of a 15º seed bead, a color A 4mm bicone crystal, and a 15º four times, leaving an 18-in. (46cm) tail. Sew through the first six beads again **(figure 1)**.

[2] Working in right-angle weave (Right-Angle Weave Basics, p. 5), pick up a 15º, a 7 x 5mm double-cone bead, two 15ºs, a color B 4mm bicone crystal, two 15ºs, a 7 x 5mm, and a 15º, and sew through the last three beads your thread exited in the previous step and the first six beads picked up in this step **(figure 2)**.

[3] Pick up a repeating pattern of a 15º, a B, and a 15º three times, and sew through the last three beads your thread exited in the previous step and all of the beads picked up in this step **(figure 3)**.

[4] Pick up a repeating pattern of a 15º, a B, and a 15º three times, and sew through the last three beads your thread exited in the previous step and the first three beads picked up in this step **(figure 4, a–b)**.

[5] Pick up a 15º, a 7 x 5mm, two 15ºs, an A, and a 15º, and sew through the 15º, 7 x 5mm, and 15º in the previous row **(b–c)**, the 15º, B, and 15º from the previous step **(c–d)**, all six beads just added **(d–e)**, and the next 15º, A, and 15º in the previous row **(e–f)**.

[6] Pick up a repeating pattern of a 15º, an A, and a 15º twice, and sew through the next two 15º–A–15º groups, and all six beads just picked up **(f–g)**.

[7] Repeat steps 4–6 19 times for a total of 21 rows, but alternate As and Bs to place them in their appropriate columns.

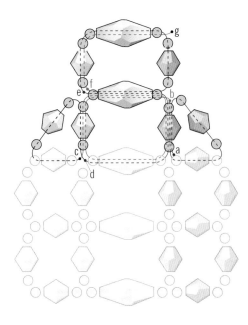

FIGURE 5

Toggle and loop

[1] Pick up a repeating pattern of a 15°, a B, and a 15° twice, and sew through the end 15°, B, and 15° in the previous row and the first three beads picked up to make a three-sided stitch (**figure 5, a–b**). Work a normal four-sided stitch in the middle column (**b–c**), then work a three-sided stitch with As (**c–d**).

[2] Sew through the beadwork to exit the top row of beads in the middle column (**d–e**), and work a four-sided stitch off of the previous stitch in the middle column (**e–f**). Sew through the beadwork to exit the top three beads (**f–g**).

[3] Pick up 15 15°s, and sew through the 15°, 7 x 5mm, and 15° in the previous row (**figure 6, a–b**), and the first eight 15°s just added (**b–c**).

[4] Pick up seven 15°s, a 7 x 5mm, and seven 15°s, and sew through the 15° your thread exited at the start of this step (**c–d**). Sew through the first seven 15°s just added, the 7 x 5mm, and the next 15° (**d–e**).

[5] Pick up a 15°, a B, and a 15°, skip the last 15°, and sew through the beads just added and the 15°, 7 x 5mm, and next 15° (**e–f**). Repeat on the other end with an A (**f–g**). Retrace the thread path a few times to reinforce the toggle. Sew through the beads connecting the toggle to the bracelet band a few times to reinforce the connection, and end the thread (Basics, p. 8).

[6] Thread a needle on the tail, and repeat steps 1 and 2 on the remaining end of the band.

[7] Pick up 25 15°s, and sew through the 15°, 7 x 5mm, and 15° your thread just exited (**figure 7**). Adjust the number of beads to fit the toggle through the loop if needed. Retrace the thread path several times to reinforce the loop, and end the thread.

DESIGNER'S NOTE:
To make the three-sided stitches lie flat at the ends of the bracelet band, try adding an extra 15° on each side of each edge 4mm bicone crystal.

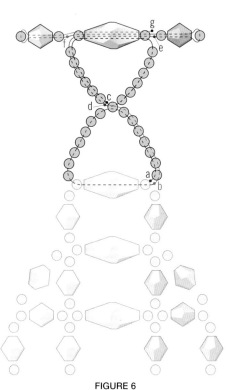

FIGURE 6

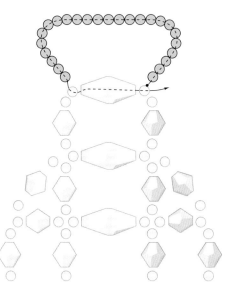

FIGURE 7

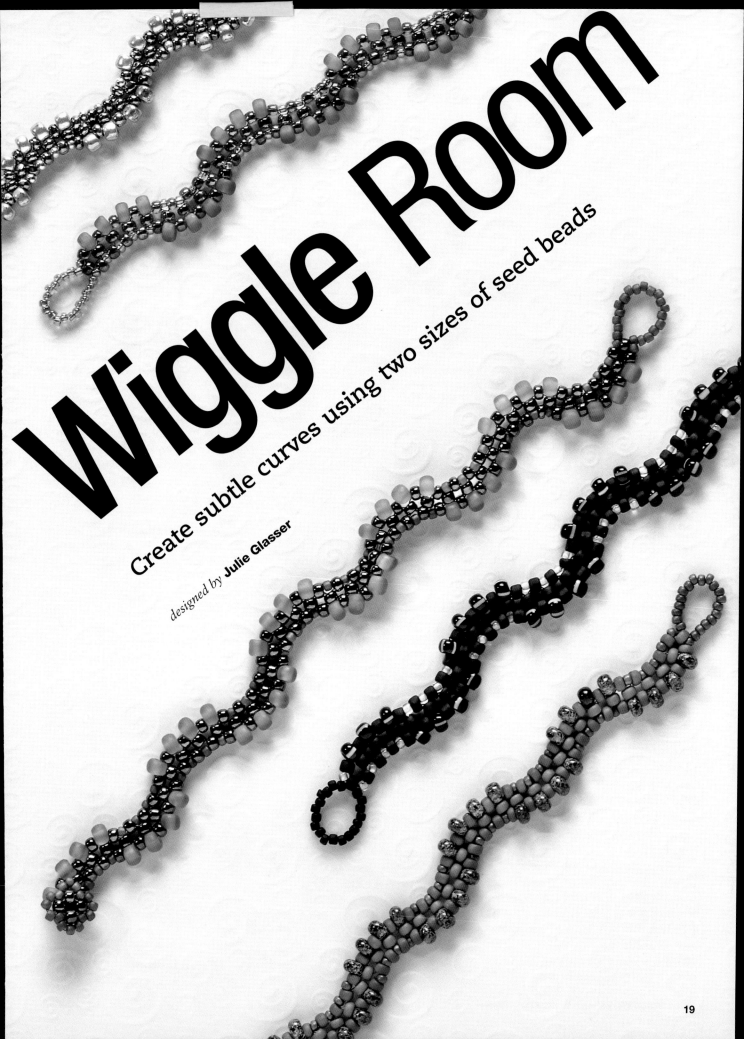

Wiggle Room

Create subtle curves using two sizes of seed beads

designed by **Julie Glasser**

MATERIALS

bracelet 6½ in. (16.5cm)

- seed beads
  - 3g 6º
  - 4g 8º
  - 2g 11º
- nylon beading thread, size D, conditioned with beeswax or Thread Heaven
- beading needles, #12

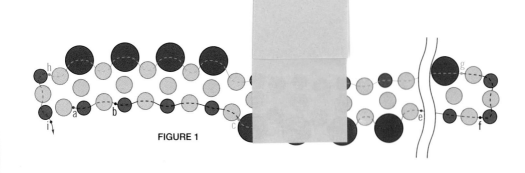

FIGURE 1

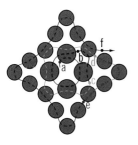

FIGURE 2

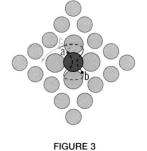

FIGURE 3

Jazz up a straight band of traditional right-angle weave by edging a base of 8º seed beads with an alternating pattern of 6º and 11º seed beads.

step by step

Base

On 3 yd. (2.7m) of conditioned thread (Basics, p. 8), pick up four 8º seed beads, leaving an 8-in. (20cm) tail. Work a strip of right-angle weave (Right-Angle Weave Basics, p. 5) 37 stitches long or to the desired length. To change the length of your bracelet, add or omit groups of four stitches to keep the edge count correct. The bracelet will shorten slightly as you add the edging. End the tail (Basics) but not the working thread.

Edging

[1] Using the working thread from the base, exit an edge 8º in the end stitch.
[2] Pick up an 11º, and sew through the next edge 8º (figure 1, a–b). Repeat to add a total of four 11ºs along the edge (b–c).
[3] Pick up a 6º seed bead, and sew through the next 8º along the edge (c–d). Repeat to add a total of four 6ºs along the edge (d–e).
[4] Repeat steps 2 and 3 for the length of the band (e–f).
[5] When you reach the end, add an 11º to each side of the end 8º (f–g).

[6] Repeat steps 2–4 along the other edge, picking up 11ºs across from the 6ºs and 6ºs across from the 11ºs (g–h), then repeat step 5 (h–i). Do not end the thread.

Button-and-loop clasp

[1] On 1 yd. (.9m) of thread, pick up four 8ºs, leaving a 10-in. (25cm) tail. Sew through the first 8º again to form a ring (figure 2, a–b).
[2] Pick up an 11º seed bead, and sew through the next 8º in the ring (b–c). Repeat to complete the round, and step up through the first 11º picked up (c–d).
[3] Pick up three 11ºs, and sew through the next 11º in the previous round (d–e).

Repeat to complete the round (e–f). Retrace the thread path through the last round, and end the working thread.
[4] Using the tail, pick up an 8º, and sew through the opposite 8º in the center ring (figure 3, a–b). Sew back through the 8º just picked up and the opposite 8º in the center ring (b–c). Retrace the thread path, and exit the new 8º.
[5] Sew through an 8º at the end of the base opposite the end your base thread is exiting, and sew through the button 8º again (photo). Retrace the thread path several times, and end the tail.
[6] Using the working thread from the base, sew through the beadwork to exit the end 8º, and pick up 19 11ºs. Sew through the end 8º again, and retrace the thread path several times to reinforce. End the working thread.

Crossing Paths

A single-strand tennis bracelet inspired an intertwining double-strand version

designed by **Lisa Twede**

Have twice as much fun when you create an optical illusion that makes two zigzagging right-angle weave bands appear to cross over and under each other. Bicone crystals add sparkle and three-dimensional flare.

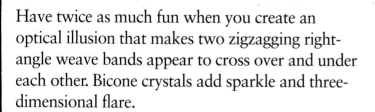
FIGURE 1

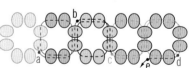
FIGURE 2

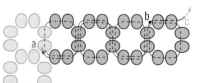
FIGURE 3

stepbystep

Band

[1] On 2 yd. (1.8m) of Fireline, pick up eight color A 11º seed beads, leaving a 6-in. (15cm) tail. Sew through the beads again to form a ring, and continue through the first four beads **(figure 1, a–b)**.

[2] Work in right-angle weave (Right-Angle Weave Basics, p. 5) as follows: one stitch with two A 11ºs, two color B 11º seed beads, and two A 11ºs **(figure 2, a–b)**; one stitch with six B 11ºs **(b–c)**; two stitches with six A 11ºs each **(c–d)**. Continue through the next two A 11ºs **(d–e)**.

[3] Turn the beadwork, and work four more right-angle weave stitches using A 11ºs **(figure 3, a–b)**. Sew through the next two A 11ºs **(b–c)**.

[4] Repeat steps 2 and 3 for the desired length of the band.

FIGURE 4

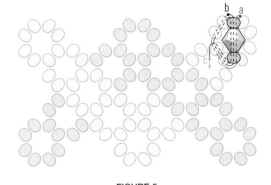

FIGURE 5

[5] Repeat step 1 using eight B 11ºs (figure 4, a–b).

[6] Pick up two B 11ºs, sew through two B 11ºs in the middle stitch of the first segment of the band, pick up two B 11ºs, and sew through the two B 11ºs your thread exited at the start of this step (b–c). Snug up the B 11ºs. Sew through the beadwork as shown (c–d).

[7] Work two more stitches using B 11ºs. Exit the edge of the last stitch (d–e).

[8] Repeat steps 6 (e–f) and 7 (f–g) for the length of the band, but alternate sewing through either the two A 11ºs or B 11ºs in the middle stitch of each subsequent segment. Do not secure or trim the threads.

Embellishment

[1] To embellish the bands, use the appropriate thread to exit at **figure 5, point a**. Pick up a color B 15º seed bead, a color B 4mm bicone crystal, and a B 15º, and sew through the beadwork as shown (a–b). Retrace the thread path (b–c). Repeat in the next color B stitch.

[2] Continue as in step 1 to embellish all the stitches, but when you get to the color A stitches, pick up a color A 15º seed bead, a color A 4mm bicone crystal, and an A 15º.

[3] With the back side of the bracelet facing up, weave through the beadwork to exit between two pairs of beads in the last stitch. Pick up a matching 15º, and sew through the next pair of 11ºs. Continue down the edge of the band. This will give the edge a crisp line.

[4] Repeat step 3, positioning 15ºs between the pairs of 11ºs in the inner openings (photo a).

[5] To attach half of the clasp, thread a needle on a thread at one end of the bands, and sew through the beadwork to exit an end bead that aligns with a clasp loop. Pick up three or four 15ºs, sew through the loop, pick up three or four 15ºs, and sew through the bead your thread exited at the start of this step (photo b). Retrace the thread path.

[6] Sew through the beadwork to exit the bead that aligns with the next clasp loop. You may also choose to anchor both loops in the same bead. Repeat step 5, sewing through the next loop of the clasp. Secure the thread in the beadwork with a few half-hitch knots (Basics, p. 8), and trim.

[7] Repeat steps 5 and 6 with the thread from the other band to attach the other loops of the clasp.

[8] End and add thread (Basics) to the other ends of the bands as needed, and repeat steps 5 and 6 to attach the other half of the clasp.

Make a pair of earrings by stitching two figure-8 sections of the design.

a

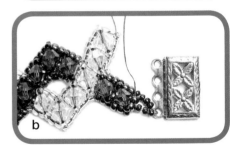

b

MATERIALS

bracelet 7 in. (18cm)
- 40 4mm bicone crystals in each of **2** colors: A, B
- 2g 11º seed beads in each of **2** colors: A, B
- 2g 15º seed beads in each of **2** colors: A, B
- four-strand clasp
- Fireline 6 lb. test
- beading needles, #12

EDITOR'S NOTE:

Allow the 15ºs added to the bracelet's edge to float between the pairs of 11ºs rather than snugging up the beads. This will help prevent the base squares from becoming distorted.

DESIGNER'S NOTE:

Place the crystals vertically or horizontally within the base squares for different looks.

Choose a deep, cool color or vibrant hue for your fire-polished beads, then pair it with seed beads that blend or contrast for maximum impact.

STACKED
Sparkle

Lacy picots surround two rows of fire-polished beads

designed by **Michelle Skobel**

Surround your favorite fire-polished beads with loops of seed beads, then embellish them for a bracelet that makes a sparkling statement with a delicate look. These bracelets work up so fast you'll have time to make them in many different colors.

stepbystep

[1] On a comfortable length of thread or Fireline, pick up 14 color A 11º seed beads and the loop of half of the clasp, leaving a 6-in. (15cm) tail. Tie the working thread and tail together with a square knot (Basics, p. 8), and sew through the next five As **(figure 1, a–b)**.

[2] Pick up a 4mm fire-polished bead, two As, and a 4mm, and sew through the last two As your thread exited, the first 4mm, and the two As just picked up **(b–c)**.

[3] Repeat step 2, working in right-angle weave (Right-Angle Weave Basics, p. 5) until the bracelet is ½ in. (1.3cm) short of the desired length. End and add thread (Basics) as needed.

[4] Pick up 12 As and the loop of the other half of the clasp, and sew through the two As your thread exited, and the first A of the new loop **(figure 2, a–b)**. Pick up six As, skip the next 4mm, and sew through the next two As **(b–c)**.

[5] Pick up seven As, skip the next 4mm, and sew through the next two As **(c–d)**. Repeat **(d–e)** to the end of the bracelet, picking up only six As in the last stitch, and sewing through an A in the loop to mirror the other clasp loop.

[6] Sew through the beads in the clasp loop, the two shared As in the first stitch, and the next A **(figure 3, point a)**. Pick up four As, skip the next 4mm, and sew through the last two As in the next loop, the two center As, and the first two As in the loop on the other side of the bracelet **(a–b)**.

MATERIALS
bracelet 7 in. (18cm)
- 54 4mm fire-polished beads
- 6g 11º Japanese seed beads, color A
- 3g 11º seed beads, color B
- clasp
- nylon beading thread, size D, or Fireline 6 lb. test
- beading needles, #12

[7] Pick up three As, skip the next 4mm, and sew through the last two As in the next loop, the two center As, and the next two As on the other side **(b–c)**. Repeat to the other end. Sew through the clasp loop on the other end, and exit a center A in the first three-A set on one edge **(figure 4, point a)**.

[8] Pick up three As, sew through the A your thread exited again, and continue through the next A **(a–b)**. Pick up an A, and sew through the next two As **(b–c)**. Repeat these two stitches along the edge, sew through the clasp loop, and repeat along the other edge.

[9] Sew through the beadwork to exit the third bead in the first picot on one edge, with your needle pointing away from the bracelet **(figure 5, point a)**. Pick up three color B 11º seed beads, and sew down through the nearest A in the next picot, the A at the base of the picot, and the next picot A **(a–b)**. Repeat **(b–c)** along the edge, and sew through the beadwork to repeat along the other edge. End the thread and tail.

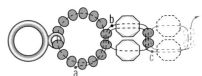

FIGURE 1

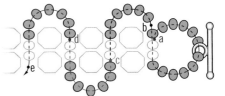

FIGURE 2

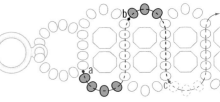

FIGURE 3

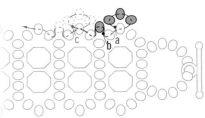

FIGURE 4

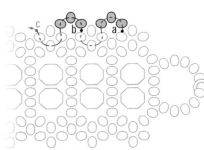

FIGURE 5

Small segments add up
to one dazzling bracelet

Brilliant Idea

designed by **Teri Dannenberg**

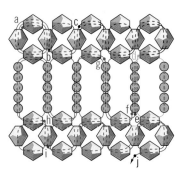

FIGURE 1

Working in sections allowed Teri to change her design as she went along, playing with color arrangements and altering the ends to get the bracelet she wanted. The easy construction of this attention-grabbing bracelet begs for you to try out your own ideas.

stepbystep

Segments

[1] On 2 yd. (1.8m) of thread, pick up four 3mm bicone crystals, leaving a 6-in. (15cm) tail. Sew through all four 3mms again to form a ring, and continue through the first two 3mms **(figure 1, a–b)**.

[2] Working in right-angle weave (Right-Angle Weave Basics, p. 5), pick up three 3mms, and sew through the 3mm your thread exited in the previous stitch. Sew through the next two 3mms **(b–c)**. Repeat three times, and sew through the next 3mm **(c–d)**.

[3] Pick up five 15° seed beads, a 3mm, and five 15°s. Sew through the 3mm your thread exited in the previous stitch and the next five 15°s **(d–e)**.

[4] Pick up a 3mm and five 15°s, sew through the next 3mm in the previous row and the five 15°s your thread exited in the previous stitch **(e–f)**, and continue through the next 3mm and the five 15°s just picked up **(f–g)**. Continue across the row in right-angle weave, and sew through the last 3mm added **(g–h)**.

[5] Pick up three 3mms, and sew through the 3mm your thread exited at the start of this stitch and the next 3mm **(h–i)**. Continue across the row in right-angle weave, and end by sewing through the bottom 3mm of the last stitch **(i–j)**.

[6] Repeat steps 1–5 to make six more individual segments. End the tails (Basics, p. 8), but do not end the working threads. Set aside.

Assembly

[1] Line up two segments one above the other, positioned with the working threads exiting as in **figure 1, point j**.

[2] Using the working thread from the top segment, pick up nine 15°s, and sew through the 3mm in the center of the next segment **(figure 2, a–b)**. Sew through four 3mms as shown **(b–c)**.

[3] Pick up nine 15°s, and sew through the second 3mm from the right in the top segment **(c–d)**. Sew through four 3mms as shown **(d–e)**. Pick up nine 15°s, and sew through the 3mm on the left end of the next segment **(e–f)**.

[4] Pick up a 15°, a 6mm bicone crystal, and a 15°, and sew through the 3mm directly opposite the 3mm your thread exited at the start of this step, in the opposite direction **(f–g)**.

[5] Flip the bracelet horizontally, and

repeat steps 2–4 to complete the join, crossing over the previous groups of 15°s. End the thread.

[6] Repeat steps 1–5 to join the remaining segments.

[7] On each end of the bracelet, add a new thread in the beadwork (Basics), and repeat steps 3 and 4 of "Segments," but pick up three 15°s for each stitch instead of five.

Clasp

[1] Add 1 yd. (.9m) of thread in the beadwork, and exit between the last two 3mms on one end of the bracelet **(figure 3, point a)**. Pick up four 15°s, and sew through the 3mm your thread exited at the start of this step and the first 15° again **(a–b)**.

[2] Pick up three 15°s, and sew through the next 3mm and four 15°s again **(b–c)**. Continue across the row in right-angle weave, exiting the end 15° **(c–d)**.

[3] Pick up a 15°, and sew back through the two 15°s that make up the top of the last right-angle weave stitch **(d–e)**. Pick up a 15°, and sew back through the next two 15°s in the previous row. Continue across the row in modified flat odd-count peyote stitch (Basics), exiting the last pair of 15°s **(e–f)**.

[4] Pick up a 15°, and sew under the thread bridge between the edge 15° and the 3mm. Sew back through the 15° just picked up **(f–g)**.

[5] Pick up two 15°s, and sew back through the next 15° in the previous row. Repeat across the row, exiting the last 15° in the previous row **(g–h)**.

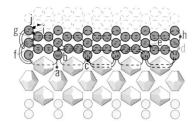

FIGURE 2

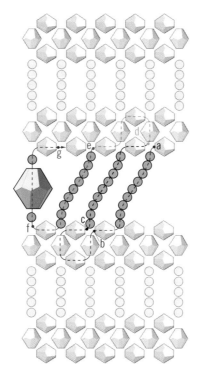

FIGURE 3

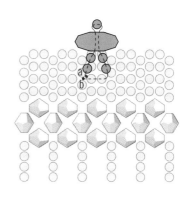

FIGURE 4

MATERIALS
bracelet 7¼ in. (18.4cm)
- 8mm rondelle
- bicone crystals
   12 6mm
   256 3mm
- 5g size 15º seed beads
- nylon beading thread, size D
- beading needles, #13

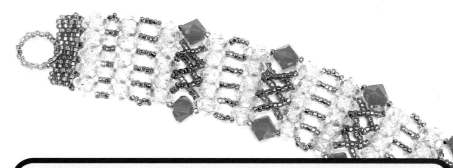

[6] To begin the next row, pick up a 15º, and sew back through the last pair of 15ºs. Repeat across the row (h–i).

[7] To make the turn, pick up a 15º, sew under the thread bridge between the last two edge 15ºs, and sew back through the 15º just picked up (i–j).

[8] Repeat steps 5–7, and then step 5 again. Sew through the peyote strip to exit the center pair of beads, three rows down (figure 4, point a).

[9] Pick up two 15ºs, an 8mm rondelle, and a 15º. Sew back through the rondelle, pick up two 15ºs, and sew through the pair of 15ºs in the strip again (a–b). Retrace the thread path several times, and end the threads.

[10] Repeat steps 1–8 on the opposite end of the strip. Pick up enough 15ºs to make a snug loop around the rondelle, and sew through the pair of 15ºs in the strip again. Retrace the thread path several times, and end the threads.

FINISHING TOUCHES

Building the bracelet in segments means it's easy to adjust the length to fit your needs. The turquoise bracelet (above) follows the instructions given and is 7¼ in. (18.4cm) long.

- To make an 8-in. (20cm) bracelet, add an eighth segment to the bracelet before finishing the ends.
- To make a 6¼-in. (15.9cm) bracelet, construct the bracelet as usual, except for step 7 of "Assembly." Instead, work an additional row of right-angle weave using 3mms on each end, as in the silver bracelet (p. 25 top).
- To make a 6½-in. (16.5cm) bracelet, construct the bracelet as usual, except for step 7 of "Assembly." Following steps 1 and 2 of "Segments," weave two single rows of right-angle weave using 3mms. Attach these small segments to each end of the bracelet, following steps 1–5 of "Assembly," and finish the ends as usual. In the gradated blues bracelet (far left and p. 25 bottom), two more rows of peyote were added to each end to increase the length to 6¾ in. (17.1cm).

Combine any of these finishing techniques to suit your taste and desired length.

Cosmic Crystals

Stitch right-angle weave saucers that are out of this world

designed by **Deborah Staehle**

MATERIALS
earrings
- 4mm bicone crystals
  20 color A
  16 color B
- **2** 2-in. (5cm) head pins
- pair of earring findings
- Fireline 6 lb. test
- beading needles, #12
- G-S Hypo Cement
- chainnose pliers
- roundnose pliers
- wire cutters

a

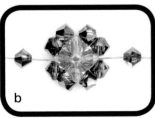

b

Double-layer beaded beads work up quickly for a sparkling set of earrings.

step by step

[1] On 1 yd. (.9m) of Fireline, pick up two color A and two color B crystals. Sew through all the crystals to form a ring. Exit the second B (figure 1, a–b).
[2] Pick up two As and a B. Sew through the B the thread is exiting and continue through the next two As and the new B (figure 2, a–b).
[3] Pick up a B and two As. Sew through the B the thread is exiting, and exit the new B (figure 3, a–b).
[4] Pick up two As. Sew through the first B from step 1 and the B from step 3. Exit the two new As (figure 4, a–b).
[5] To start the second layer, pick up two Bs, and sew through the two As from

step 4 (figure 5, a–b). Sew through the two new Bs and the two As from step 3 (b–c).
[6] Pick up a B, and sew through the previous B and the two As from step 3. Exit the new B (c–d). Pick up a B, sew through the two As from step 2 and the previous B. Exit the new B (d–e).
[7] Sew through the next two As from step 1 and the first B

added in step 5. Exit the last B added (e–f). The tails should be next to each other.
[8] Tie the tails into a square knot (Basics, p. 8). Dot the knot with glue, let the glue dry, and trim the tails.
[9] On a head pin, string an A, the crystal saucer, and an A (photo a). Make the first half of a wrapped loop (Basics). Slide the earring finding into the loop, and finish the wraps.
[10] Make a second earring to match the first.

> **EDITOR'S NOTES:**
> - **For a bracelet, make three crystal saucers and string them horizontally (photo b) on flexible beading wire, stringing assorted beads and spacers between the crystal saucers to reach the desired length.**
> - **Deborah also uses a crossweave approach to create these earrings; contact her (see p. 87) for instructions.**

FIGURE 1

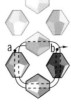
FIGURE 2

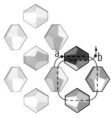
FIGURE 3

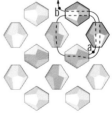
FIGURE 4

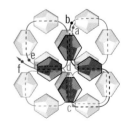
FIGURE 5

Spring
Snowflakes

**Enjoy the icy look of
snowflakes year-round
with crystals**

designed by **April Bradley**

Use this easy technique to create an elegant chain of crystal snowflakes that drapes dramatically around your neck.

step by step

[1] On 2 yd. (1.8m) of Fireline, pick up a repeating pattern of a 3mm silver bead and a 6mm bicone crystal four times. Tie the beads into a ring with a square knot (Basics, p. 8), and sew through the next 3mm in the ring **(figure 1)**.

[2] Pick up a 4mm bicone crystal, a 3mm, and a 4mm. Sew through the 3mm your thread exited at the start of this step and the next 6mm and 3mm in the ring **(figure 2, a–b)**.

[3] Pick up three 4mms, and sew through the 3mm your thread exited at the start of this step and the next 6mm and 3mm in the ring **(b–c)**.

[4] Repeat steps 2 and 3 **(c–d)**, then sew through the next four beads and the following 4mm and 3mm **(d–e)**.

[5] Pick up a repeating pattern of a 6mm and a 3mm three times, then pick up a 6mm. Sew through the 3mm your thread exited at the start of this step and the next 6mm and 3mm **(figure 3, a–b)**.

[6] Repeat steps 3 and 4 **(b–c)**.

[7] Repeat steps 5 and 6 until you have 22 6mm units. End the threads (Basics).

[8] Add 30 in. (76cm) of thread (Basics) on one end of the necklace, leaving a 6-in. (15cm) tail and exiting the inside top 4mm **(figure 4, point a)**.

[9] Pick up a 3mm, a 6mm, and a 3mm. Sew through the next 4mm, 3mm, and 4mm at the top of the next 6mm unit **(a–b)**. Repeat **(b–c)** until you reach the other end of the necklace. End the threads.

[10] Cut a 3-in. (7.6cm) piece of 22-gauge wire. Make the first half of a wrapped loop (Basics), and slide the loop through the end 3mm on one end of the necklace. Complete the wraps **(photo a)**. Make the first half of a wrapped loop above the wraps, attach one half of the clasp, and complete the wraps.

[11] Repeat step 10 on the other end of the necklace **(photo b)**.

MATERIALS
necklace 18 in. (46cm)
- bicone crystals
  109 6mm
  178 4mm
- **132** 3mm silver beads
- clasp
- 6 in. (15cm) 22-gauge wire
- Fireline 6 lb. or 8 lb. test
- beading needles, #12
- chainnose pliers
- roundnose pliers
- wire cutters

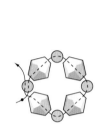

FIGURE 1

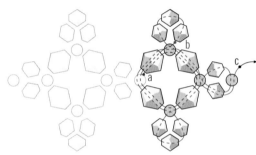

FIGURE 2

FIGURE 3

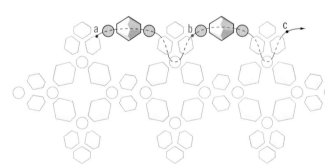

FIGURE 4

a

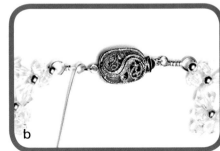

b

Make a BIG Crystal Splash

An unusual clasp component sparkles
on a band of rippling right-angle weave

designed by **Marcia DeCoster**

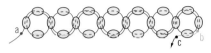

FIGURE 1

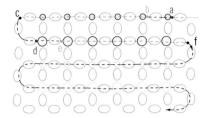

FIGURE 2

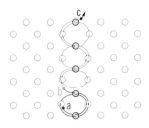

FIGURE 3

This band looks complicated, but it has only two layers. The base layer is stitched with 3mm beads, so it works up quickly. The seed bead embellishments added in the second layer create the rippled texture.

step by step

Band

[1] On a comfortable length of unconditioned thread, pick up four 3mm fire-polished beads, leaving a 6-in. (15cm) tail. Sew through the first three beads again to form a ring. Picking up three 3mms per stitch, work a total of seven right-angle weave stitches (Right-Angle Weave Basics, p. 5 and **figure 1, a–b**).

[2] Sew through the next edge 3mm **(b–c)** to begin the next row. Continue working rows of right-angle weave until the band is 1½ in. (3.8cm) longer than the desired finished length, ending and adding thread (Basics, p. 8) as needed. As you work, keep your stitches very loose **(photo a)**. The beadwork will be pulled together when the embellishment is added. A band 45 rows long will make a 7¾-in. (19.7cm) bracelet. End the working thread and tail.

[3] Add a comfortable length of thread at one end of the band, and, sewing toward the inner rows, position the needle so it exits a corner 3mm **(figure 2, point a)**.

[4] Pick up a 15º seed bead, and sew through the next 3mm in the row **(a–b)**. Repeat across the row, adding a total of six 15ºs **(b–c)**.

[5] Sew through the next edge 3mm and the following 3mm in the next row **(c–d)**. Pick up an 8º seed bead, and sew through the next 3mm **(d–e)**. Repeat across the row, adding a total of six 8ºs **(e–f)**.

[6] Repeat steps 4 and 5 for the length of the band to embellish it with alternating rows of 15ºs and 8ºs. Don't embellish the last two rows at the end of the band **(photo b)**. The rivoli and hook-and-eye clasp will be attached here. End the working thread and tail.

Clasp

[1] On 1 yd. (.9m) of thread, pick up four 15ºs, leaving a 10-in. (25cm) tail. Sew through the first three beads again to form a ring. Working in right-angle weave, stitch a strip with 15ºs that is a bead or two short of the rivoli's circumference. Work two or three more rows.

[2] To sew the strip into a short tube, connect the first and last rows: Pick up a 15º, and sew through the edge 15º in the first row. Pick up a 15º, and sew through the four beads in the stitch **(figure 3, a–b)**. Continuing in a right-angle weave thread path, add one 15º per stitch to complete the connection **(b–c)**.

[3] Thread a needle on the 10-in. (25cm) tail, and sew through the beads on the edge of the tube, pulling them together so they are snug. Secure the tail, but don't trim.

[4] Place the rivoli in the tube with the faceted side facing up **(photo c)**.

[5] With the working thread exiting a bead in the top round of the tube, sew through the edge beads in the round to cinch them as close to the rivoli as

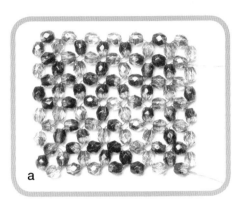

a

b

c

MATERIALS
bracelet 7¾ in. (19.7cm)
- 14mm or 20mm square or round Swarovski rivoli
- **750** 3mm Czech fire-polished beads
- seed beads
  4g 8º
  2g 11º
  2g 15º
- small hook-and-eye clasp
- nylon beading thread, size B
- beading needles, #12

possible. If the beads are spaced far apart, add beads as needed for a better fit. If you're using a round rivoli, you may work a round of peyote stitch (Basics and **photo d**), and then sew through the peyote round again to cinch up the beads.

[6] Embellish the beaded bezel as desired by stitching 15ºs and/or 11ºs between the horizontal beads in a round on the bezel's edge **(photo e)**. Repeat around the bezel, adding embellishment rounds as desired. Secure the thread, and weave through to the bottom round of the bezel.

[7] Stitch the hook half of the clasp to the bottom round of the bezel **(photo f)**. Secure the working thread, and trim.
[8] On the opposite side of the rivoli, stitch the bezel to the unembellished surface at the end of the band by sewing back and forth through the bezel and the center three 3mms in the second row **(photo g)**. Retrace the thread path several times, and end the thread.
[9] Working on the other end of the band, stitch the eye half of the clasp to the 8ºs on each side of the center 3mm in the second row **(photo h)**. End the thread.

EDITOR'S NOTE:
Stitching the base of 3mms loosely is critical. If the base is stitched too tightly, the 8ºs won't fit between the 3mms.

This narrower version of the bracelet began with a 14mm round rivoli and five right-angle weave stitches instead of seven.

Stripes
Forever

Teardrop-shaped fringe beads accent a striped bracelet with row-by-row color changes

designed by **Phyllis Dintenfass**

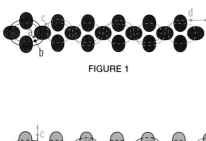

FIGURE 1

FIGURE 2

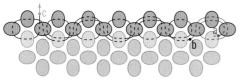

FIGURE 3

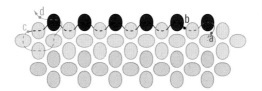

FIGURE 4

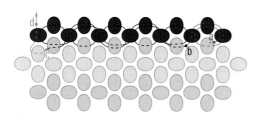

FIGURE 5

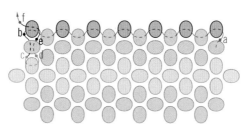

FIGURE 6

MATERIALS

bracelet 7 in. (18cm)

- 33–36 3mm drop beads, color A
- 11º seed beads
  5g color A
  4g color B
- button for clasp (optional)
- Fireline 6 lb. test
- beading needles, #12
- drinking straw (optional)

In this variation on right-angle weave, offset, interlocking rows create a band with interesting texture that is enhanced by the addition of drop beads in the center. Either sew a peyote toggle to the top of the band or the shank of a button into the band as you stitch for a complementary clasp.

stepbystep

Band

[1] On 2 yd. (1.8m) of Fireline, pick up four color A 11º seed beads (figure 1, a–b), leaving a 24-in. (61cm) tail. Sew through the four As again and continue through the next A to form a ring (b–c). Snug up the beads.

[2] Work five stitches of right-angle weave (Right-Angle Weave Basics, p. 5), using As (c–d).

[3] Pick up a color B 11º, and sew through the next three beads in the end stitch (figure 2, a–b). Pick up a B and sew through the next A (b–c). Continue across the row, adding a B between each pair of As (c–d). Pick up a B, sew

through the end A in the previous row, and sew through the B again (d–e). Flip the beadwork after every row to be in position to work the next row.

[4] Pick up three Bs, and sew through the last B added in step 3 and the three Bs just added (figure 3, a–b). Continue working in right-angle weave across the row (b–c).

[5] Pick up an A, and sew through the next B (figure 4, a–b). Continue across the row, adding an A between each pair of Bs (b–c). Sew through the end stitch of Bs in the previous row and the last A added in this step (c–d).

[6] Pick up three As, and sew through the last A added in the previous step and the three As just added

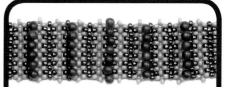

EDITOR'S NOTE:
In the original bracelet, the middle row of drops is slightly off-center. To make it symmetrical, modify the center stripe of the band (step 12) by replacing the middle As in the cluster with drops (photo above). Use seven, rather than six, drops across the stripe. Begin the stripe by repeating step 5 of the band. To sew the clusters, pick up As and drops in the following order: a drop, an A, and a drop. For the remaining five clusters, alternate picking up a drop and an A, and an A and a drop.

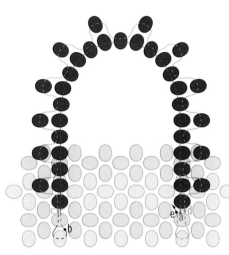

FIGURE 7

(figure 5, a–b). Continue across the row (b–c). Sew through the adjacent end B in the previous row and the end A of the last stitch (c–d).

[7] Repeat steps 3–6, ending with steps 3 and 4, to sew seven pairs of alternating A and B stripes with the following change: In step 3, after adding each row of single Bs (figure 6, a–b), secure the ends by sewing through the end A below the B just added (b–c), the top B of the last stitch in the previous B stripe (c–d), back through the A (d–e), and back through the B just added (e–f).

[8] Repeat steps 5 and 6, but in step 6 pick up As and 3mm drop beads in the following order: an A, a drop, and an A. For the remaining five stitches, alternate picking up an A and a drop, and a drop and an A.

[9] Stitch a stripe of Bs, a stripe of As, and a stripe of Bs.

[10] Repeat step 8.

[11] Stitch a stripe of Bs, a stripe of As, and a stripe of Bs.

[12] Repeat step 5, but use drops instead of As. Repeat step 6.

[13] Repeat steps 11 and 12 twice.

[14] Repeat step 7 to sew seven pairs of alternating stripes of As and Bs. Check the fit of your bracelet. The ends of the band should meet when you wrap it around your wrist. To adjust the length, add or remove alternating stripes of As and Bs to both ends to reach the desired length. End the thread (Basics, p. 8).

Button clasp

If you plan to use a button for the clasp, you can either work it in as you stitch the base, positioning it approximately half the length of the button away from the end, or add it after the base is completed. To add it afterward, sew through the beadwork to exit where the button needs to be attached. Pick up five or six 11ºs and the shank of the button, and sew through a nearby bead. Retrace the thread path several times, and end the thread. Proceed to "Clasp loop" to complete the bracelet.

Toggle clasp

[1] To make a toggle bar, string a stop bead (Basics) on 1 yd. (.9m) of Fireline, and leave a 6-in. (15cm) tail.

[2] Pick up 12 As, and, working in flat, even-count peyote stitch (Basics), sew a strip with three As on each straight edge.

[3] In the next row, replace four to six As in the center of the row with drops. Continue working in peyote stitch until the strip has seven As on each straight edge.

[4] Zip up the strip (Basics) to form a tube. To stiffen the tube, cut a drinking straw to the length of the toggle bar. Cut the straw lengthwise, roll it tightly, and slide it inside the tube.

[5] To taper the ends of the tube, sew through the beadwork to exit an edge bead. Pick up an A, sew through the next A, and exit the following A. Continue around until you've added seven As. Sew through all the As added in this step to snug them up. Repeat at the other end of the tube.

[6] Sew through the beadwork and exit the fourth A from the end in the row opposite the drops.

[7] Sew two right-angle weave stitches to form a tab. Attach the toggle bar to the bracelet by sewing into the second stripe from the end. Reinforce the tab, and end the thread.

Clasp loop

[1] To form the loop, thread a needle on the tail, and sew through the beadwork to exit at figure 7, point a. Pick up enough As (approximately 25) to fit around the toggle bar or button. Sew through the base to point b.

[2] Anchor the thread by sewing through the adjacent B and back through the A just exited (b–c).

[3] Sew back through the last A in the loop and embellish the loop with peyote stitch, using As (c–d).

[4] Sew into the base A where you began the loop and back through the adjacent B and the A (d–e). Sew back through the loop to reinforce the stitching, and end the thread.

Seed Bead
Loops Add Drama

Create a scalloped
edge to change the
shape of this bracelet

designed by **Connie Blachut**

EDITOR'S NOTE:
Some 11º seed beads are a little larger than others, and if you use a hex-cut bead or another shape, you may have to change the amount of beads you use for each loop of the scalloped edge.

Substantial, yet comfortable to wear, this right-angle weave band can be dressed up with a center row of just about any 4mm beads. Make a casual version with pearls and a seed bead edging, or add glitz with sparkling crystals and hex-cut beads.

stepbystep

Base

[1] On 3 yd. (2.7m) of Fireline, pick up eight 8º seed beads, leaving a 10-in. (25cm) tail. Sew through the first four 8ºs again (figure 1, a–b).

[2] Pick up six 8ºs, sew back through the last two 8ºs your thread just exited (b–c), and continue through four new 8ºs (c–d).

[3] Pick up six 8ºs, and sew through the last two 8ºs your thread exited (d–e) and all six new 8ºs (e–f).

[4] To begin the next row, pick up six 8ºs, sew through the two 8ºs your thread just exited, and continue through the first two new 8ºs (f–g).

[5] Pick up four 8ºs, and sew through the middle two 8ºs in the previous row and the last two 8ºs your thread exited in the previous stitch (g–h). Continue through the four new 8ºs (h–i), and sew through the last two 8ºs in the previous row (i–j).

[6] Pick up four 8ºs, and sew through the last four beads your thread just exited. Continue through the four new 8ºs (j–k).

[7] To work the next row, flip your work over, and repeat steps 4–6 (k–l).

[8] Repeat steps 4–7 until you reach the desired length. Make your bracelet so the number of rows is divisible by 3. Set the thread aside.

[9] Pick up the tail, and sew through the first row of beads as shown in figure 2, a–b. Sew through one loop of the clasp and through the next two 8ºs (b–c and photo a). Sew through the other loop of the clasp and the next two 8ºs (c–d). End the tail (Basics, p. 8).

[10] Repeat step 9 on the other end with the working thread, but before securing the thread, exit at figure 3, point a. Pick up an 8º, and sew through the next two 8ºs along the side of the base (a–b). Pick up an 8º, and sew through the next two 8ºs (b–c). Continue around the base, reinforcing the clasp loops instead of adding 8ºs when you reach the ends (c–d). Exit at point e.

a

b

Scalloped edge

[1] Secure 2 yd. (1.8m) of Fireline (Basics) in the beadwork, and exit at figure 4, point a.

[2] Pick up six 11ºs. Sew through four 8ºs as shown (a–b). Push the first loop onto the top of the bracelet.

[3] Pick up six 11ºs, skip one of the 8ºs on the side, and sew through the next four 8ºs (figure 5, a–b). Push the new loop on top of the first, making sure the loops form a spiral from the front of the bracelet to the back as you add loops.

[4] Repeat step 3 seven times for a total of nine loops, which make up the first scallop. To make the next scallop, position the first loop to lie on top of the bracelet (photo b). Repeat along the edge to make ten scallops. Repeat on the other edge, and end the threads.

Center

[1] Add 1 yd. (.9m) of Fireline in the beadwork, exiting at figure 6, point a.

[2] Pick up an 11º, a pearl or crystal, and an 11º. Sew through the next two center 8ºs in the same direction so the new beads lie across the center stitch diagonally (a–b). Repeat along the center row of the base, and end the thread.

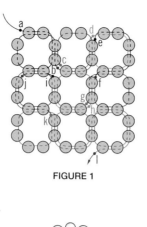

FIGURE 1

FIGURE 2

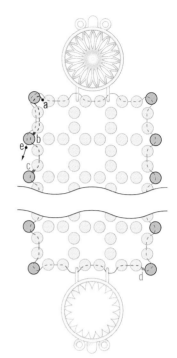

FIGURE 3

FIGURE 4

FIGURE 5

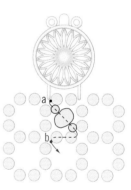

FIGURE 6

To make the scallops symmetrical instead of parallel, change the orientation of the scallops on one edge by stitching each one so it starts in the back and wraps around to the front.

Scalloped Lace

Create a glamorous necklace of gentle curves

designed by **Donna Pagano Denny**

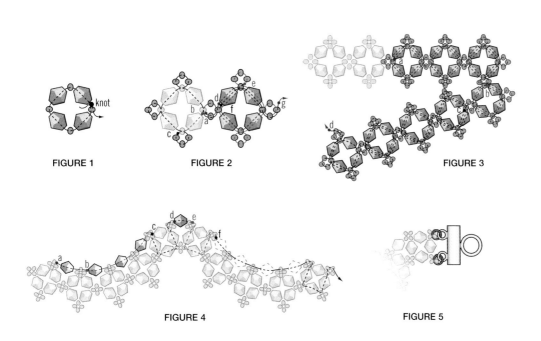

FIGURE 1

FIGURE 2

FIGURE 3

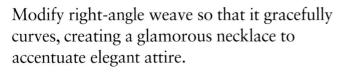

FIGURE 4

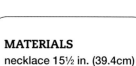

FIGURE 5

Modify right-angle weave so that it gracefully curves, creating a glamorous necklace to accentuate elegant attire.

stepbystep

[1] On 3 yd. (2.7m) of Fireline, pick up a repeating pattern of a 15º seed bead and a color A 4mm bicone crystal four times, leaving a 6-in. (15cm) tail. Tie the beads into a ring with a surgeon's knot (Basics, p. 8). Sew through the first 15º again (figure 1).

[2] To create a picot, pick up three 15ºs, sew through the 15º your thread is exiting (figure 2, a–b), and continue through the next 4mm and 15º (b–c).

[3] Repeat step 2 three times, and sew through the first two 15ºs added in step 2 (c–d).

[4] Pick up a 4mm and a 15º three times, then pick up another 4mm. Sew through the 15º your thread is exiting and the next 4mm and 15º again (d–e).

[5] Work a picot off each 15º (e–f), and sew through the beadwork to exit the tip of the picot opposite the previous unit (f–g).

[6] Repeat steps 4 and 5 three times, but after the third repeat, exit the tip of the picot adjacent to the previous connection point (figure 3, a–b).

[7] Repeat steps 4 and 5, but in step 5, exit the tip of the picot adjacent to the previous connection point (b–c).

[8] Repeat steps 4 and 5 to complete four more units, but in the last repeat, exit the tip of the picot adjacent to the previous connection point, making sure to exit the same edge as in steps 6 and 7 (c–d).

[9] Repeat steps 7 and 8 seven times, ending and adding thread (Basics) as needed. Test the fit and work another five-unit section if desired. If your working thread is less than 24 in. (61cm) long, end the threads on both ends of the necklace, and add 24 in. of thread on one end.

[10] The edge with the adjacent connection points is the lower or outer edge of the necklace. Sew through the beadwork to exit the center 15º on the inner edge picot in the first unit (figure 4, point a).

[11] Pick up a color B 4mm bicone crystal, and sew through the center 15º in the next unit (a–b). Repeat three times (b–c), and sew through the beads in the next unit to exit the center 15º (c–d).

[12] Pick up an A, and sew through the center 15º in the next edge picot (d–e). Sew through the beadwork as shown (e–f).

MATERIALS
necklace 15½ in. (39.4cm)
- 4mm bicone crystals
  209 color A
  40 color B
- 5g 15º seed beads
- lobster claw clasp
- 2 two-to-one findings
- 4 3mm inside-diameter 20-gauge jump rings
- 2 3–4mm split rings
- Fireline 6 lb. test
- beading needles, #12
- 2 pairs of pliers

[13] Repeat steps 11 and 12 to the end of the beadwork. End the thread.

[14] Open a jump ring (Basics), and attach one of the picots at the end of the necklace to one of the loops of a two-to-one finding. Repeat with a second jump ring and the second loop of the same two-to-one finding (figure 5). Repeat on the other end of the necklace. Attach a split ring to the remaining loop of each two-to-one finding. Attach the lobster claw clasp to one of the split rings.

DESIGNER'S NOTE:
For a more casual style, you can use 3 or 4mm crystal pearls in place of the 4mm crystals.

Crystal Tiles

Four stitches are the foundation for this bracelet with custom toggle clasps

designed by **Geneva Beck**

EDITOR'S NOTE:
To make a pair of earrings, complete two right-angle weave sections. Sew a soldered jump ring to a corner, and attach the earrings to earring findings.

Crystals sit atop grids of right-angle weave like miniature glittering mosaics. Combine ladder and square stitch with netting to create clever double toggles.

stepbystep

Base

[1] On 3 yd. (2.7 m) of Fireline, leaving an 18-in. (46cm) tail, use 11º seed beads to stitch a ladder (Basics, p. 8) two beads wide and three rows long (figure 1, a–b).
[2] Pick up six 11ºs, sew through the last two 11ºs your thread just exited, and continue through the first four new 11ºs (b–c). Working in right-angle weave (Right-Angle Weave Basics, p. 5), repeat for a total of four stitches (c–d).

[3] Using two 11ºs per stitch, work two ladder stitches (d–e).
[4] Work four right-angle weave stitches (e–f).
[5] Repeat steps 3 and 4 for the desired bracelet length, ending with two ladder stitches.
[6] Continuing in the established pattern, work a second column, sharing the side beads of the right-angle weave sections (figure 2). Work a total of four columns.
[7] At one end, position the thread to exit at **figure 3, point a**. Pick up an 11º, and sew through the two end

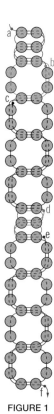

FIGURE 1

11ºs of the next ladder (a–b). Repeat twice (b–c).

[8] Using 11ºs, work a row of square stitch (Basics) off the previous row (c–d).

[9] Using one 11º per stitch, work five ladder stitches (d–e). Using two 11ºs per stitch, work 10 stitches of modified square stitch off the last two 11ºs in the ladder (e–f).

[10] Sew through the next 11º (f–g). Using one 11º per stitch, work three ladder stitches, and attach the last ladder stitch to the first row of square stitch (g–h). Secure the thread in the beadwork with a few half-hitch knots (Basics), but don't trim.

[11] Using the tail, repeat steps 7–10 on the opposite end of the bracelet.

Embellishment

[1] Add a new thread (Basics) to the base, and exit the first right-angle weave stitch at one end.

[2] Pick up a 15º seed bead, a 4mm bicone crystal, and a 15º, cross the stitch diagonally, and sew through the beads on the opposite side of the stitch and the next two beads (figure 4, a–b). Repeat across this row of stitches, then repeat across the next row (b–c). Repeat for the remaining two rows of the right-angle weave section. End the thread (Basics).

[3] Repeat steps 1 and 2 for the remaining right-angle weave sections.

Toggles

[1] On 2 yd. (1.8m) of Fireline, pick up a pattern of an 11º and a 4mm three times, leaving a 6-in. (15cm) tail. Sew through all the beads again, and tie them into a ring with a square knot (Basics). Sew through the next 11º (photo a).

[2] Pick up five 11ºs. Skip the next 4mm, and sew through the following 11º. Repeat twice, and step up through the first three 11ºs added in this step (photo b).

[3] Pick up a 4mm, and sew through the center 11º in the next stitch (photo c). Repeat twice to complete the round.

[4] Repeat steps 2 and 3 until you have a total of seven 4mm rounds, then sew through the beadwork to exit a center 11º (photo d). Work a ladder stitch using one 11º, work four ladder stitches using two 11ºs per stitch, then work one more stitch using one 11º.

[5] Attach the toggle to the base by sewing through the fifth 11º in the first square stitch row on one end of the bracelet (photo e). Retrace the thread path to reinforce the connection, and end the working thread and tail.

[6] Make a second toggle on the other end of the bracelet, but attach it to the fifth 11º from the other edge so the toggles are offset slightly when clasped.

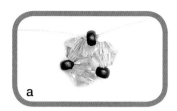
a

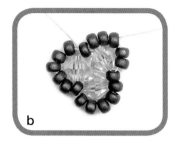
b

c

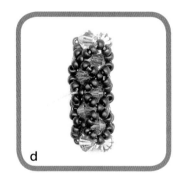
d

e

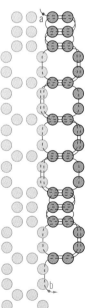
FIGURE 2

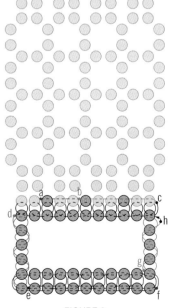
FIGURE 3

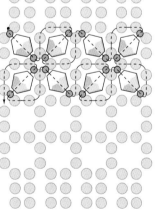

FIGURE 4

The number of crystals in these bracelets could be overpowering, but a monochromatic palette creates a subtle flash that's more eye-catching than over-the-top.

Crystalline Bracelet

A sprinkling of crystals shimmers in a modified right-angle weave band

designed by **Abby Cobb**

In pale aqua, this airy bracelet of seed beads and matching crystals brings to mind wintery images of sparkling ice and snowflakes. If you'd rather think of spring, try a brighter color, like lilac. Whichever season you choose, keep your tension loose for a more fluid-looking bracelet.

stepbystep

Clasp button

[1] On 1½ yd. (1.4m) of Fireline, pick up four 11º seed beads and, leaving a 6-in. (15cm) tail, tie them into a ring using a square knot (Basics, p. 8). Sew through the next 11º in the ring (**figure 1, a–b**).

[2] Pick up an 11º, and sew through the next 11º in the ring (**b–c**). Repeat to add three more 11ºs around the ring, and step up through the first 11º added (**c–d**).

[3] Pick up two 11ºs, and sew through the second 11º added in step 2 (**d–e**). Repeat to add two 11ºs per stitch around the ring, and step up through the first two 11ºs added (**e–f**).

[4] Pick up an 11º, a 4mm bicone crystal, and an 11º (**figure 2, a–b**). Skip the last 11º, and sew back through the 4mm. Pick up an 11º, and sew through the next pair of 11ºs from step 3 (**b–c** and **photo a**). Pull tight to form a crystal picot.

[5] Repeat step 4 to add three more crystal picots. After adding the fourth picot, sew through only one 11º (**c–d**).

[6] Pick up six 11ºs, and sew through the 11º at the end of the picot you just completed (**figure 3, a–b**).

[7] Pick up six 11ºs, and sew through the three 11ºs at the base of that picot (**b–c** and **photo b**).

[8] Continue around the loop you've just created and the three 11ºs at the base of the previous picot (**c–d**).

[9] Work as in step 6 to begin a loop around the next crystal. Pick up four 11ºs, and sew through the last two 11ºs of the previous loop, the three 11ºs at the base of the picot, and the next two 11ºs of the loop just created (**d–e**).

[10] Make a loop around the fourth crystal (**e–f**).

[11] Sew through the first two 11ºs of the first loop. Complete the loop around the fourth crystal, and continue through the loop just created (**f–g**).

[12] Exiting at **point g**, pick up two 11ºs. Skip the next bead of the loop your thread is exiting and the adjacent bead of the next loop, and sew through the next seven 11ºs of the next loop (**photo c**), exiting the loop's second-to-last bead. (Rotate your beadwork to match the figure, and exit where **point g** would be if it were on each loop.)

[13] Repeat step 12 around the button, adding two 11ºs where each pair of loops joins. Don't pull too tightly, or you'll distort the button. Retrace the thread path, and end the threads (Basics).

FIGURE 1

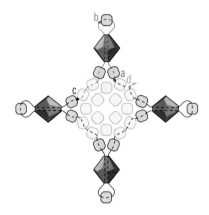

FIGURE 2

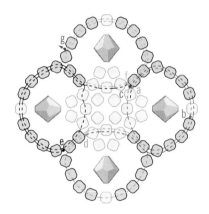

FIGURE 3

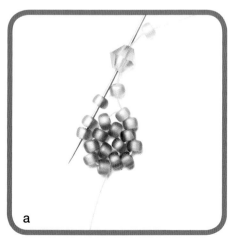

a

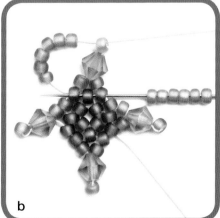

b

c

45

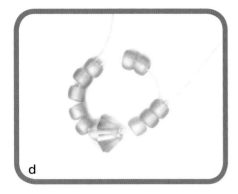

d

e

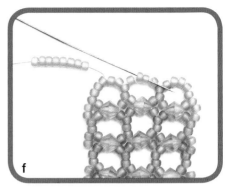

f

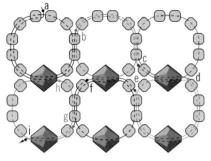

FIGURE 4

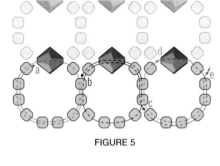

FIGURE 5

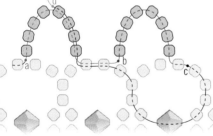

FIGURE 6

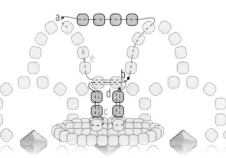

FIGURE 7

Base

[1] Thread a needle on a comfortable length of Fireline or doubled nylon beading thread. Leaving a 15-in. (38cm) tail, pick up five 11ºs, a 4mm, and five 11ºs. Sew through all the beads except the last two again (**photo d** and **figure 4, a–b**), and pull tight to form a ring.

[2] Work in right-angle weave (Basics) as follows: Pick up seven 11ºs, a 4mm, and an 11º. Sew through the last two beads your thread exited in the previous ring, and continue through the next six 11ºs in the second ring (**b–c**).

[3] Pick up an 11º, a 4mm, and seven 11ºs. Sew through the two side 11ºs in the second ring, and continue through the next 11º and 4mm (**c–d**).

[4] Pick up four 11ºs, a 4mm, and four 11ºs. Sew through the 4mm your thread exited, and continue through all the beads you just picked up except for the last one (**d–e**).

[5] Pick up an 11º and sew through the next 4mm in the previous row (**e–f**). Pick up four 11ºs, a 4mm, and an 11º.

Sew through the next three 11ºs, the 4mm, and the next three 11ºs (**f–g**).

[6] Pick up an 11º, a 4mm, and four 11ºs, and sew through the next 4mm in the previous row (**g–h**). Pick up an 11º, and sew through the next three 11ºs and the 4mm (**h–i**).

[7] Repeat steps 4–6 until you have 23 rows of crystals, ending and adding thread (Basics) as needed.

[8] Pick up 10 11ºs. Sew through the 4mm in the previous row and the next nine 11ºs (**figure 5, a–b**).

[9] Pick up an 11º. Sew through the next 4mm in the previous row. Pick up seven 11ºs, sew through the two side 11ºs of the previous ring, the first 11º picked up in this ring, the 4mm, and the next three 11ºs (**b–c**).

[10] Pick up seven 11ºs, and sew through the next 4mm in the previous row (**c–d**). Pick up an 11º, and sew through the next eight 11ºs (**d–e**).

[11] Pick up two 11ºs, skip two 11ºs, and sew through the next two 11ºs on the edge (**photo e**). Repeat, adding two

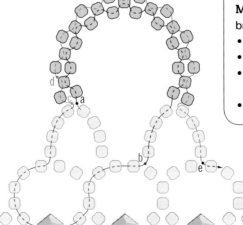

FIGURE 8

MATERIALS

bracelet 7 in. (18cm)

- **73** 4mm bicone crystals
- **9g** 11º seed beads
- Fireline 4 lb. test, or nylon beading thread, size B
- beading needles, #12

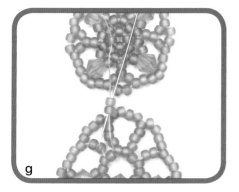

g

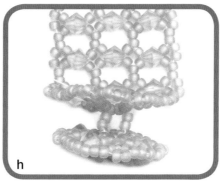

h

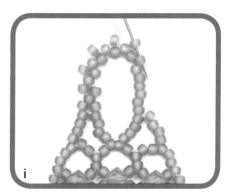

i

11ºs between each pair of stitches until you've reached the other end.

[12] Sew through the beadwork and repeat step 11 on the other side, adding thread as needed. Secure the working tail in the beadwork with a few half-hitch knots, but don't trim the tails.

Clasp

[1] With the working thread, sew through the beadwork to exit at **figure 6, point a**. Pick up eight 11ºs, and sew through the top two 11ºs in the middle ring (**a–b** and **photo f**).

[2] Pick up eight 11ºs, and sew through the top right 11º on the outside ring (**b–c**). Continue through the beadwork to exit the center of the first loop added in step 1 (**c–d**).

[3] Pick up four 11ºs, and sew through the inner four 11ºs added in step 2 (**figure 7, a–b**).

[4] Sew through the center two 11ºs of the middle ring in the previous row, pick up two 11ºs, and sew through a bead near the center of the clasp button (**b–c**).

[5] Sew back through the two 11ºs you just picked up (**photo g**) and the two 11ºs of the middle ring (**c–d**).

[6] Pick up two 11ºs, and sew through an adjacent center 11º of the button. Sew back through the two 11ºs just picked up, the two middle-ring 11ºs, and into the 11ºs picked up in step 1 (**d–e**). Pull tight (**photo h**). Retrace your thread path to reinforce the join, and end the thread.

[7] Thread a needle on the tail at the other end of the bracelet, and repeat steps 1 and 2, exiting **figure 8, point a**.

[8] Pick up 19 11ºs, and sew through the inside four 11ºs from step 2 (**a–b**). Sew through the beadwork as shown (**b–c**).

[9] Pick up an 11º, skip an 11º, and sew through the second 11º in the loop (**c–d**). Continue working in peyote stitch (Basics), adding one 11º per stitch around the loop (**photo i**). End by sewing through the outside four 11ºs from step 2 (**d–e**). Retrace the thread path around the clasp loop, and end the thread.

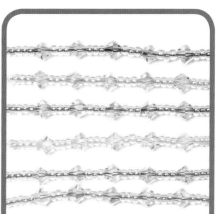

EDITOR'S NOTE:
Because this bracelet features a cushioning 11º seed bead on both sides of each sharp crystal, your thread isn't as likely to be cut as it would in other designs, so you can use nylon thread instead of Fireline. Take advantage of the opportunity to pair clear crystals and beads with colored thread (use it doubled) for a touch of color. The samples shown here are all sewn with the same 11ºs and crystals; the only difference is the thread.

For a secure closure, create a loop just large enough to accommodate the button while it's gently folded. Once clasped, the stitched button will then lie flat again.

Crystals Across

Criss-cross a bugle-bead base with seed beads, pearls, and crystals

designed by **Julie Walker**

Two layers of embellishments top a right-angle weave base, creating a sparkling adornment for your wrist.

FIGURE 1

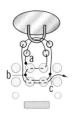

FIGURE 2

stepbystep

Base
[1] On 3 yd. (2.7m) of thread, pick up four 8º seed beads, and leave a 12-in. (30cm) tail. Working in square stitch (Basics, p. 8), add a second row of four 8ºs off the first row of 8ºs **(figure 1, a–b)**.
[2] Exiting the last 8º in the row, pick up an 11º, a 6mm bugle bead, and an 11º. Sew through the previous row of 8ºs, the first 11º, and the 6mm bugle **(b–c)**.
[3] Pick up an 11º, an 8º, an 11º, a 12mm bugle bead, an 11º, an 8º, and an 11º. Sew through the 6mm bugle, and the next four beads **(c–d)**.
[4] Continue working in right-angle weave (Right-

Angle Weave Basics, p. 5) by following the pattern **(d–e)** and alternating two 12mm bugles with three 6mm bugles until the bracelet is 1 in. (2.5cm) shorter than the desired length. End with one 6mm bugle so it matches the beginning of the base.
[5] Pick up an 11º, four 8ºs, and an 11º. Sew through the last bugle, the first 11º just picked up, and the 8ºs. Work a second row of 8ºs in square stitch. Exit the second 8º from the end in the last row of 8ºs **(figure 2, point a)**.
[6] Pick up an 11º, a button, and an 11º and sew through the middle two 8ºs in the last row **(a–b)**. Sew through the middle two 8ºs in the previous row **(b–c)**.

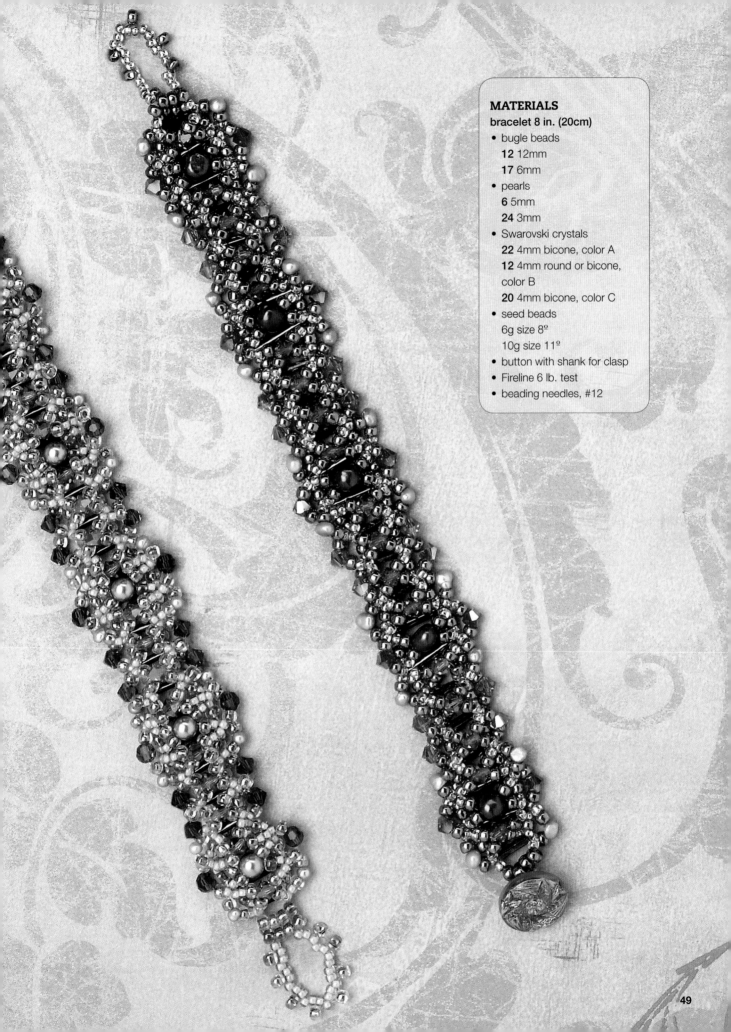

MATERIALS
bracelet 8 in. (20cm)
- bugle beads
  12 12mm
  17 6mm
- pearls
  6 5mm
  24 3mm
- Swarovski crystals
  22 4mm bicone, color A
  12 4mm round or bicone, color B
  20 4mm bicone, color C
- seed beads
  6g size 8º
  10g size 11º
- button with shank for clasp
- Fireline 6 lb. test
- beading needles, #12

[7] Pick up an 11º, sew through the button, and pick up an 11º. Sew through the middle two 8ºs your thread just exited. Retrace the thread path a few times to reinforce the button, and end the working thread (Basics).

[8] Using 12-in. (30cm) tail, and exit the second 8º from the edge in the end row of 8ºs on the other end **(figure 3, point a)**. Pick up enough 11ºs (approximately 25) to make a loop large enough to accommodate your button. Sew through the middle two 8ºs in the last row again **(a–b)**.

[9] Sew through the first 11º in the loop, pick up an 8º, skip two 11ºs in the loop, and sew through the next 11º **(b–c)**. Repeat around the loop, and sew through the middle two 8ºs in the last row **(c–d)**. Retrace the thread path to reinforce the loop, and end the tail.

Embellishment
[1] Thread a needle on each end of 2 yd. (1.8m) of thread. Center the thread in the first bugle on one end of the base.

[2] On one needle, pick up an 11º, an 8º, a 4mm color A bicone crystal, an 8º, and two 11ºs. Sew through the next bugle so the beads lie across the opening of the stitch **(figure 4, a–b)**.

[3] On the other needle, pick up an 11º and an 8º. Sew through the A from the previous step **(d–e)**. Pick up an 8º and two 11ºs, and sew through the next bugle so the beads form an X over the opening **(e–f)**.

[4] Repeat step 3 across the band, substituting a 5mm pearl for the 4mm crystal between each pair of 12mm bugles **(b–c and f–g)**. End the threads.

[5] Repeat step 1.

[6] On both needles, pick up an 11º, an 8º, a 3mm pearl, an 8º, and an 11º. Cross the needles through the next bugle in the base **(figure 5, a–b and d–e)**.

[7] Continue adding loops along the edges of the base by repeating step 6, but alternate the bead pattern of pearls, color B bicone or round crystals, and color C bicone crystals **(b–c and e–f)** until you reach the opposite end. End the threads.

FIGURE 3

FIGURE 4

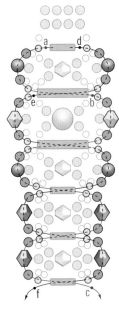

FIGURE 5

EDITOR'S NOTE:
Because there are slight differences in the size of seed beads, you may have to adjust the number of 11ºs you use in the embellishment, especially when transitioning from a 12mm bugle to a 6mm bugle and vice versa.

Embellishing only
three sides of the base
creates a domed bead.

Bedecked
Baubles

Create sparkling
right-angle weave
beaded beads

designed by **Mia Gofar**

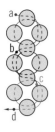

FIGURE 1

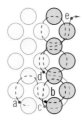

FIGURE 2

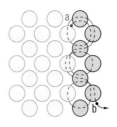

FIGURE 3

FIGURE 4

FIGURE 5

FIGURE 6

EDITOR'S NOTE:
Make an embellished bead with 3mm crystals and fire-polished beads instead of 4mms and with 15º seed beads instead of 11ºs. You can also embellish all four sides of the base.

a

b

c

MATERIALS

necklace 17 in. (43cm)

- 8mm Swarovski round crystal, color C
- 4 8mm round or bicone crystals, color B
- 8 6mm bicone crystals or rondelles, color B
- Swarovski bicone crystals
  8 8mm, color C
  8 5mm, color D
  80 4mm, color C
  55 4mm, color B
  26 4mm, color E
- 84 4mm round fire-polished beads, color A
- 1g 11º seed beads
- lobster claw clasp
- 2 in. (5cm) chain to accommodate lobster claw clasp
- 2-in. (5cm) 22-gauge head pin
- 2 crimp beads
- 2 crimp covers (optional)
- Fireline 6 lb. test
- flexible beading wire, .014
- beading needles, #12
- chainnose pliers
- crimping pliers
- roundnose pliers
- wire cutters

stepbystep

Base

[1] On 2 yd. (1.8m) of Fireline, pick up four 4mm color A fire-polished beads, leaving an 8-in. (20cm) tail. Working in right-angle weave (Right-Angle Weave Basics, p. 5), sew through the first three As again (figure 1, a–b).
[2] Pick up three As, and continue in right-angle weave (b–c). Repeat for the next stitch (c–d).
[3] Sew through the next three As of the last stitch (figure 2, a–b), and begin a second row of right-angle weave off the first: Pick up three As, and sew through the bead the thread just exited (b–c). Continue through the next three As (c–d). Complete the row as shown (d–e).
[4] Work a third row of right-angle weave off the second row (figure 3, a–b).
[5] Fold the beadwork in half, and work a fourth row of right-angle weave, connecting the first and third rows (figure 4, a–b).
[6] Retrace the thread path to reinforce the four As on

each end. Exit an end bead (photo a). Don't trim the working thread.
[7] Make a total of three right-angle weave bases.

Embellishment

[1] Pick up a color B 4mm bicone crystal, an 11º seed bead, and a B 4mm. Sew through the opposite A (figure 5, a–b). Repeat twice down the vertical column of right-angle weave stitches.
[2] Pick up a color C 4mm bicone, and sew through the 11º from the previous stitch (figure 6, a–b). Pick up a C 4mm and sew through the opposite A (b–c). Repeat to complete the column.
[3] Pick up an 11º, and sew through the next end A (photo b).
[4] Repeat steps 1–3 twice to complete two more columns.
[5] Sew through the horizontal rows of As, adding an 11º between the columns as in step 3. End the thread (Basics, p. 8). Trim the working thread, and secure the tail in the same manner.
[6] Repeat steps 1–5 to embellish the remaining bases.

Assembly

[1] On 22 in. (56cm) of flexible beading wire, string a crimp bead and lobster claw clasp. Go back through the crimp bead, and crimp it (Basics). Trim the excess wire.
[2] String five C 4mms, six color E 4mm bicones, five C 4mms, seven E 4mms, three C 4mms, a color B 6mm bicone or rondelle, a color D 5mm bicone, a color C 8mm bicone, a color B 8mm bicone or round, a C 8mm bicone, a D 5mm, a B 6mm, a beaded bead, a B 6mm, a D 5mm, a C 8mm, a B 8mm, a C 8mm, a D 5mm, and a B 6mm.
[3] String an embellished bead, and then string the remaining crystals to mirror the first half of the necklace.
[4] String a crimp bead and 2 in. (5cm) of chain. Go back through the crimp bead and crimp it. Trim the excess wire. Use crimp covers to cover the crimps if desired.
[5] On a head pin, string a C 8mm round crystal and a B 4mm. Make the first half of a wrapped loop (Basics). Attach the dangle to the chain, and finish the wraps (photo c).

Zig Zag Bangle

Turn a craft store find into a beaded bangle

designed by **Lisa Kan**

MATERIALS

bangle outside diameter 3 in. (7.6cm)
- 11º seed beads
  10g color A
  2g color B
- 5g 11º triangle beads
- 2g 15º seed beads
- 3-in. (7.6cm) brass craft ring
- Fireline 6 lb. test
- beading needles, #12

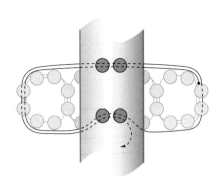

FIGURE 1

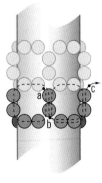

FIGURE 2

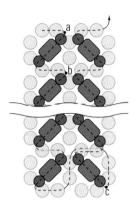

FIGURE 3

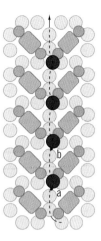

FIGURE 4

When Lisa spotted a 3-in. (7.6cm) brass ring normally used for macramé, it lit up a mental lightbulb for her. She slid the ring onto her wrist and began imagining what stitch would surround this form, transforming it from an ordinary object into a fun beaded bangle. Alternating the direction of the embellishment creates the zigzag effect of these bangles.

stepbystep

In the how-to photos, color B 11° seed beads were used to make each new stitch easier to see. The base is tubular right-angle weave (Right-Angle Weave Basics, p. 5) with six stitches in each round.

[1] On 4 yd. (3.7m) of Fireline, pick up eight color A 11° seed beads, leaving a 6-in. (15cm) tail. Tie the beads into a ring with a surgeon's knot (Basics, p. 8), and sew through the first six As again.

[2] Pick up six As, and, working in right-angle weave (Right-Angle Weave Basics), sew through the last two As in the previous stitch and the first four As just picked up. Repeat this step three times.

[3] Wrap the strip around the brass craft ring, and join the strip into a ring with a right-angle weave (**figure 1** and

a

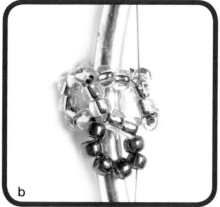

b

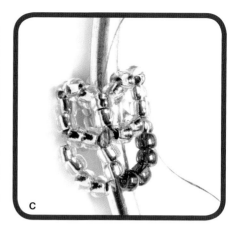

c

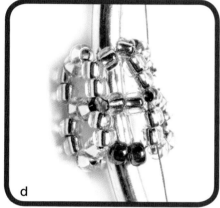

d

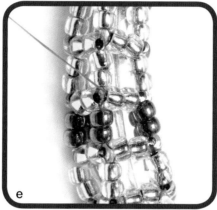

e

f

photo a) to complete the first horizontal round of stitches.

[4] Work the next round off of the previous one, picking up six As for the first stitch (figure 2, a–b and photo b), four As for the next four stitches (b–c and photo c), and two As for the last stitch in the round (photo d). Continue working in tubular right-angle weave, ending and adding thread (Basics) as needed to cover the bangle until there is a two-bead gap between the first and last rounds.

[5] Carefully line up the vertical rounds, and join the ends (photo e). End the working thread and tail.

[6] Add 2 yd. (1.8m) of Fireline to the beadwork, exiting two 11°s in a vertical round (figure 3, point a).

[7] Pick up a 15° seed bead, an 11° triangle bead, and a 15°. Sew through the next two 11°s in the vertical round (a–b and photo f). Repeat, adding a 15°, a triangle, and a 15° to the entire vertical round.

[8] Sew through the As to exit the next vertical round as shown (b–c), and repeat step 7. The 15°, triangle, and 15° should cross the stitch in the opposite direction as the ones in the previous vertical round.

[9] Repeat step 8 to embellish the remaining vertical rounds, always crossing the stitch in the opposite direction as the previous round and ending and adding thread as needed.

[10] To add a color B 11° seed bead between the stitches in the vertical rounds, exit two As (figure 4, point a). Pick up a B, and sew through the next two 11°s (a–b). Repeat to complete the round. Add Bs between the stitches in the remaining vertical rounds. End the thread.

EDITOR'S NOTES:
- If the craft ring you purchased has a smaller gauge than the one Lisa used, or if your beads are slightly bigger, the embellishment won't work as well. To compensate for the difference, try wrapping waxed linen around the craft ring until the beadwork fits well around the ring.
- If you have a hard time fitting your color B 11°s between the stitches in the inner rounds when you add them to the bangle, try adding B 11°s to the three outer rows and 15°s to the rows on each side of the 11°s, and then skipping the inner row.

What's Your Bangle?

Construct a sturdy bangle with a right-angle weave base

designed by **Shelley Nybakke**

> **EDITOR'S NOTE:**
> While the round metal seed beads give the bangle a lot of its structure and weight, it can be made with other beads. For example, the base could be created with 3mm Swarovski pearls (as above) or regular size 8⁰ seed beads. The right-angle weave will buckle a lot more using either of these options, so as you add the embellishments, use 11⁰s for the inner rounds to help keep the shape. The 3mm crystals should work the same either way.

a

b

c

d

The base of this bangle is made by stitching four rounds of 8º seed beads in right-angle weave and sewing them into a tube while stitching the fifth round. Metal seed beads lend strength to the bracelet's structure, but the same bracelet can be created using regular seed beads or even pearls.

step by step

Base

[1] Pick up four 8º seed beads on 3 yd. (2.7m) of doubled Fireline, leaving a 10-in. (25cm) tail. Sew through the first three 8ºs again, forming a ring (figure 1, a–b).

[2] Pick up three 8ºs and sew through the bead your needle is exiting. Sew through the next two beads (b–c).

[3] Working in right-angle weave (Right-Angle Weave Basics, p. 5), repeat step 2 until you have a strip long enough to fit loosely around the largest part of your hand. Work a right-angle stitch to join the first and last stitches together (figure 2, a–b).

[4] Work a second round off the first in right-angle weave. Start by picking up three 8ºs and sewing through the 8º your thread is exiting. Sew through the first 8º added in the new round (figure 3, a–b).

[5] Pick up two 8ºs, and sew through the next edge 8º from the previous round (b–c). Sew through the three beads in this stitch and the next edge 8º in the previous round (c–d).

[6] Continue working in right-angle weave, picking up two 8ºs per stitch, for the remainder of the round. Work the last stitch in right-angle weave, adding one 8º (figure 4, a–b).

[7] Work two more rounds of right-angle weave (photo a).

[8] To stitch the cuff into a tube, work another round of right-angle weave, connecting the first round to the fourth round: Exit an edge 8º in round 4, pick up an 8º, and sew through the corresponding edge 8º in the first round. Pick up an 8º and sew through all four 8ºs again (photo b). Continue around, adding one 8º per stitch, and end the threads (Basics, p. 8).

Embellishment

As you examine the base, you'll see that there are rows of beads whose holes line up in long rows around the circumference of the band. You'll add your embellishment beads in the spaces between these beads, working one round at a time.

[1] Add 2 yd. (1.8m) of Fireline in the beadwork (Basics), exiting an 8º on an inner round. Pick up an 8º, and sew through the next 8º in the round (photo c). Continue for the remainder of the round, and then repeat for the other inner round.

[2] For the outer rounds, add a 3mm bicone crystal between each pair of 8ºs in the round (photo d). Repeat to add 3mms along the three outer rounds.

[3] Reinforce the rounds if needed to strengthen the bangle, and end the threads.

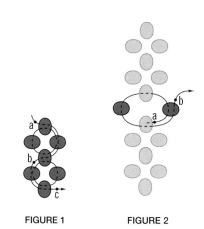

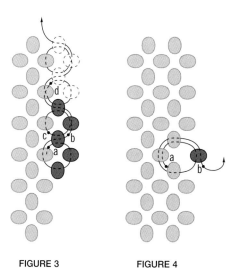

FIGURE 1

FIGURE 2

FIGURE 3

FIGURE 4

MATERIALS

bangle circumference 7¾ in. (19.7cm)

- **150** 3mm bicone crystals
- 25–30g 8º metal or round seed beads
- Fireline 10 lb. test
- beading needles, #10

Metal rings linked by seed
beads mimic traditional
chain mail, a style Cindy has
dubbed BeadMaille™.

Chain *of* Rings

Use seed beads in right-angle weave to create a stitched variation of a European chain mail pattern

designed by **Cindy Thomas Pankopf**

Small decorative rings and chains of seed beads come together for a necklace that unites two techniques. Linking the rings through the loops of right-angle weave creates a look that mimics traditional chain mail patterns but includes the color and texture of seed beads.

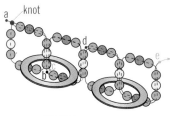

FIGURE 1

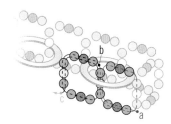

FIGURE 2

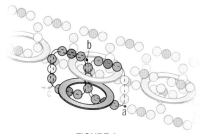

FIGURE 3

step by step

Row 1

[1] On a comfortable length of Fireline, pick up a color A 11º seed bead, a color B 11º seed bead, two As, a color C 11º seed bead, and an A. Repeat the six-bead pattern, and pick up a 9mm ring. Tie the beads into a ring with a square knot (Basics, p. 8), leaving a 10-in. (25cm) tail. Sew through the first six beads again **(figure 1, a–b)**.

[2] Pick up an A, a B, two As, a C, two As, a B, and an A, and sew through the 9mm and the last three beads in the previous stitch again **(b–c)**. Continue through the first six beads picked up in this step **(c–d)**.

[3] Pick up nine 11ºs following the established color pattern and a 9mm. Working in right-angle weave (Right-Angle Weave Basics, p. 5), sew through the end three 11ºs in the previous stitch and the first six beads just added. Repeat step 2 **(d–e)**.

[4] Repeat step 3 until your chain has 36 9mms, ending and adding thread (Basics) as needed.

[5] Work one stitch of right-angle weave following the established color pattern, but do not add a 9mm.

Row 2

[1] Pick up nine 11ºs following the established color pattern, and sew through the last 9mm added in the previous row, the last three 11ºs in the previous stitch, and the first six 11ºs just added **(figure 2, a–b)**.

[2] Pick up nine 11ºs, and sew through the same 9mm, the last three 11ºs in the previous stitch, and the first six 11ºs just added **(b–c)**.

[3] Continue working in right-angle weave, sewing through the 9mms added in the previous row as in steps 1 and 2, until you have stitched the second row through a total of 11 9mms.

[4] Begin adding 9mms to the second row: Pick up nine 11ºs in the established color pattern and a 9mm, and sew through the next 9mm in the previous row and the last three 11ºs in the previous stitch. Continue through the first six 11ºs added in this step and the two 9mms **(figure 3, a–b)**. Pick up nine 11ºs in the established pattern, and work a stitch, sewing through both 9mms **(b–c)**.

MATERIALS
necklace 17 in. (43cm)
- 12 x 18mm outside-diameter (OD) decorative metal oval
- **61** 9mm OD decorative metal rings
- 11º seed beads
  10g color A
  5g each of **2** colors: B, C
- clasp
- Fireline 6 lb. test
- beading needles, #10 or #12

[5] Repeat step 4 to add a total of 14 9mms in the second row. Depending on how you stitch, the new 9mms may sit above or below the 9mms added in the first row, but they must be consistent.

[6] Work the remainder of the row as in steps 1 and 2 without adding new 9mms.

[7] Join the ends of the first and second row with a regular stitch, as you did at the other end: Pick up an A, a B, and an A, and sew through the three edge 11ºs in the first stitch of the first row. Pick up an A, a B, and an A, and sew through the three end 11ºs at the end of the second row. End the thread.

Row 3

[1] On a comfortable length of Fireline, pick up an A, a B, two As, a C, two As, a B, and an A, and sew through the three 11ºs that are shared by the stitches between the second and third 9mm in the second row. Tie the working thread and tail together with a surgeon's knot (Basics), and sew through the first six 11ºs added in this step **(figure 4, a–b)**.

[2] Work as in step 4 of "Row 2" **(b–c)** to add a total of 10 9mms to the third row. Connect the third row to the

second as in step 1: Pick up an A, a B, and an A, and sew through the A, C, and A connecting the corresponding stitching in row 2. Pick up an A, a B, and an A, and sew through the beads your thread exited in the third row.

Center dangle

[1] Sew through the beadwork to exit the A, C, and A between the fifth and sixth 9mm in the third row. Pick up two As, a B, three As, a C, three As, a B, two As, and a 9mm. Sew through the A, C, and A your thread exited and the first eight 11ºs added in this step **(figure 5, a–b)**.

[2] Work a nine-bead stitch following the established color pattern **(b–c)**. Work another stitch, picking up the 12 x 18mm oval **(c–d)**. Sew back through the beadwork to exit the A, C, and A in the single 9mm **(d–e)**.

[3] Pick up two As, a B, three As, a C, three As, a B, and two As, and sew through one of the two nearest 9mms in the third row and through the three 11ºs your thread exited at the start of this step **(figure 6, a–b)**. Repeat with the other 9mm **(b–c)**. End the thread.

Clasp

[1] Using the tail at one end of the necklace, pick up two As, a B, two As, the loop of half of the clasp, two As, a B, and two As. Sew through the three 11ºs at the end of the first row **(figure 7)**. Retrace the thread path, and end the thread.

[2] Add 12 in. (30cm) of thread to the other end of the necklace if necessary, and repeat step 1 to attach the other half of the clasp.

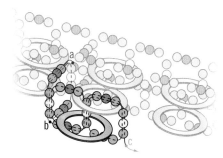

FIGURE 4

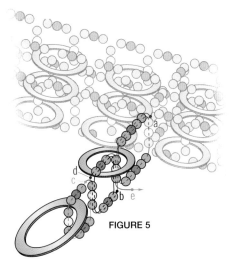

FIGURE 5

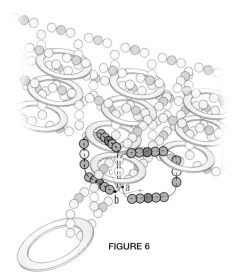

FIGURE 6

A hammered clasp matches the finish of the 9mm rings.

FIGURE 7

Pearls and Pagodas

Subtle structures define a right-angle weave band

designed by **Cathy Lampole**

MATERIALS

bracelet 7½ in. (19.1cm)

- **58** 6mm pearls
- **44** 3mm pearls
- **76** 4mm bicone crystals
- 5–7g 15º Japanese seed beads
- clasp
- nylon beading thread, size D
- beading needles, #12

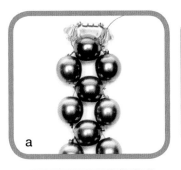

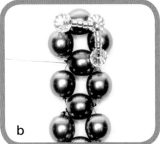

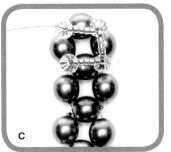

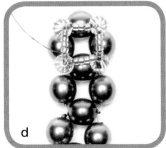

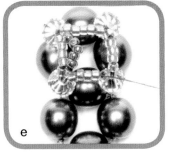

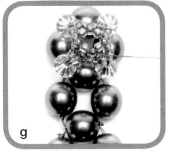

Right-angle weave provides all sorts of opportunities for embellishment. Take full advantage of that in this bracelet, building up from the base row and filling all the spaces in between.

stepbystep

[1] On 3 yd. (2.7m) of thread, leave a 6-in. (15cm) tail, and use 6mm pearls to make a right-angle weave strip (Right-Angle Weave Basics, p. 5) that is 19 stitches long.

[2] With the thread exiting the end 6mm in the last stitch, pick up a 4mm bicone crystal, five 15º seed beads, and a 4mm. Sew through the end 6mm and the first 4mm again **(photo a)**.

[3] Working in right-angle weave, pick up five 15ºs and a 4mm, and sew through the next 6mm in the stitch, the 4mm your thread just exited, the five 15ºs and 4mm just added, and the next 6mm in the stitch **(photo b)**.

[4] Pick up a 4mm and five 15ºs. Sew through the previous 4mm and 6mm, through the next 6mm in the stitch, and the adjacent 4mm that was added in step 2 **(photo c)**.

[5] Pick up five 15ºs, and sew through the 4mm added in the previous stitch, the 6mm below the 15ºs just added, the next 4mm, and the first four 15ºs of the set just added **(photo d)**.

[6] Pick up five 15ºs, and sew through the last three 15ºs your thread exited at the start of this step and the center three 15ºs in the next stitch **(photo e)**.

[7] Pick up four 15ºs, and sew through the end 15º in the previous stitch, the center three 15ºs your thread just exited, and the center three 15ºs in the next stitch. Repeat.

[8] Sew through the end 15º in the first stitch, pick up three 15ºs, and sew through the end 15º in the last stitch and the three center 15ºs your thread just exited. Step up through the first three 15ºs in the new stitch **(photo f)**.

[9] Pick up a 15º, and sew through the center 15º in the next stitch. Repeat three more times **(photo g)**. Retrace the thread path through the

top ring of 15ºs, and sew through the beadwork to exit the 6mm connecting the next right-angle weave stitch.

[10] To work each subsequent "pagoda," exit the connecting 6mm, and repeat steps 2–9, ending and adding thread (Basics, p. 8) as needed. End with at least 1 yd. (.9m) of thread.

[11] To attach the clasp, exit an edge 6mm in the last stitch. Pick up two 3mm pearls, three 15ºs, half of the clasp, and three 15ºs. Sew back through the two 3mms and the end 6mm **(photo h)**. Pick up two 3mms and three 15ºs, sew through the same half of the clasp, and pick up three 15ºs. Sew back through the two 3mms, retrace the thread path several times, and exit an edge 6mm next to the end 6mm.

[12] Pick up a 3mm, and sew through the next 6mm on the same edge **(photo i)**. Repeat along this edge until you reach the last 6mm. Sew through the end 6mm, and repeat step 11 to attach the other half of the clasp on this end. Then continue adding 3mms along the remaining edge. End the threads.

Right-Angle Weave in the Round

designed by **Barb Switzer**

Create a stunning circular pendant with a variation on right-angle weave

A variation of right-angle weave lets you create a circular shape that you can embellish with crystals and seed beads.

stepbystep

Pendant
Base
[1] On 2 yd. (1.8m) of Fireline, pick up an 8° seed bead, two 11°s, an 11° cylinder bead, a 4mm bicone crystal, a cylinder, and two 11°s **(figure 1, a–b)**, leaving an 8-in. (20cm) tail. Sew through the 8°, two 11°s, and the cylinder **(b–c)**, pulling the beads into a ring.
[2] Pick up a 4mm, a cylinder, and three 11°s. Sew through the two 11°s and the cylinder from the previous step **(c–d)**. Then sew through the 4mm, the cylinder, and the first two 11°s just added **(d–e)**.
[3] Pick up an 8°, two 11°s, a cylinder, and a 4mm. Sew through the cylinder and two 11°s from the previous step **(e–f)**, then sew through the 8°, two 11°s, and the cylinder just added **(f–g)**.
[4] Repeat steps 2 and 3 until you have 15 rings. To complete the base, pick up a 4mm, and sew through the cylinder and the two 11°s from the first ring **(figure 2, a–b)**. Pick up an 11°, and sew through the two 11°s and the cylinder from the last ring. Sew through the 4mm just added **(b–c)**.

Embellishment
[1] Pick up a 15°, an 11°, a 3mm bicone crystal, an 11°, and a 15° **(figure 3, a–b)**. Sew through the 11° opposite the 4mm. Pick up a 15° and an

11º, and sew back through the 3mm (b–c). Pick up an 11º and a 15º, and sew through the 4mm again (c–d). Flip the base over, and repeat on the back.

[2] Pick up a 15º, a cylinder, and a 15º (d–e). Sew back through the cylinder, pick up a 15º, and sew through the next 4mm (e–f).

[3] Repeat steps 1 and 2 around the ring. On every other ring, sew through the 8º opposite the 4mm instead of an 11º. When you complete the circle, sew through the next 15º, cylinder, and 15º (figure 4, a–b).

[4] Pick up a 3mm, a 15º, and a 3mm. Sew through the next 15º (b–c). Repeat around the base.

[5] Reinforce the outer edge with a second thread path, and exit a 15º.

[6] Pick up an 11º and 15 15ºs. Sew back through the 11º and into the 15º on the outer edge to make a loop. Reinforce the loop with a second thread path. End the working thread and tail (Basics, p. 8).

Necklace

[1] Center the pendant and two cylinders on 20 in. (51cm) of flexible beading wire. Secure one end of the wire with a Bead Stopper or tape.

[2] String a 4mm, a 3mm, a cylinder, an 11º, and a cylinder. Repeat, adding three 11ºs instead of one.

[3] String a 4mm, a 3mm, and a 4mm. String a cylinder, five 11ºs, and a cylinder.

[4] Repeat step 3 six times, altering the number of 11ºs added each time, as follows: seven 11ºs, nine 11ºs, 11 11ºs, 11 11ºs, nine 11ºs, and seven 11ºs. String a 3mm, a crimp bead, a 4mm, and half of a clasp. Go back through the 4mm and the crimp bead. Crimp the crimp bead (Basics), and trim the tail.

[5] Remove the Bead Stopper or tape, and repeat steps 2–4 on the other side of the pendant with the other half of the clasp.

MATERIALS

pendant
- bicone crystals
  16 4mm
  64 3mm
- seed beads
  16 8º
  1g 11º
  1g cylinder beads
  2g 15º or 14º
- Fireline 6 lb. test
- beading needles, #13

necklace 16 in. (41cm)
- bicone crystals
  34 4mm
  20 3mm
- 5g 11º seed beads
- 3g 11º cylinder beads
- clasp
- **2** crimp beads
- flexible beading wire, .014
- crimping pliers
- wire cutters
- Bead Stopper or tape

FIGURE 1

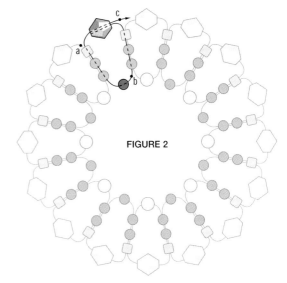

FIGURE 2

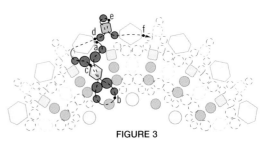

FIGURE 3

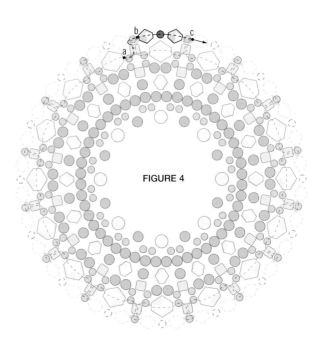

FIGURE 4

EDITOR'S NOTE:
You can substitute other shapes for the 3mm and 4mm bicone crystals; just make sure that they have large enough holes for several thread passes.

Victorian
Sparkle

Learn to bezel with right-angle weave

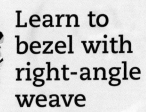

designed by **Julie Walker**

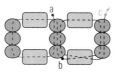

FIGURE 1

MATERIALS

pendant 1⅜–1½ in. (3.5–3.8cm)

- 27–30mm Swarovski pointed-back stone (1202) or chessboard stone (2035) focal element
- 15–18mm crystal or cubic zirconia briolette
- 6 5–7mm crystal or cubic zirconia briolettes
- bicone crystals
  14–17 4mm
  32–35 3mm, color A
  8–10 3mm, color B
- **6** 2mm round crystals
- 3g 8º hex-cut seed beads
- 2g 11º seed beads
- 3g 15º Japanese seed beads
- Fireline 6 lb. test
- beading needles, #12 or #13

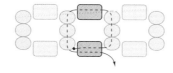

FIGURE 2

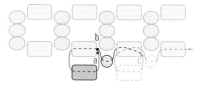

FIGURE 3

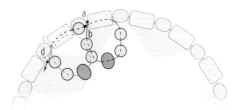

FIGURE 4

FIGURE 5

Surround a large crystal stone with layers of seed beads, bicones, and briolettes.

stepbystep

[1] On 3 yd. (2.7m) of Fireline, center three 11º seed beads, an 8º hex-cut seed bead, three 11ºs, and an 8º. Tie the working thread and tail together with a square knot (Basics, p. 8), and sew through the first three 11ºs again **(figure 1, a–b)**.

[2] Pick up an 8º, three 11ºs, and an 8º, and sew through the three 11ºs your thread exited at the start of this step again. Continue through the next 8º and three 11ºs **(b–c)**.

[3] Continue stitching in right-angle weave (Right-Angle Weave Basics, p. 5), until you have a strip of beads that just fits or nearly fits around your focal stone. Join the ends into a ring by picking up an 8º, sewing through the first three 11ºs, picking up an 8º, and sewing through the last three 11ºs again. Sew through the first 8º again **(figure 2)**.

[4] Pick up an 8º, and sew through the 8º your thread exited again **(figure 3, a–b)**. Pick up a 15º seed bead, and sew through the next 8º **(b–c)**. Repeat these two stitches around the ring, then sew through all the 8ºs in the new round to snug up the beads. Secure the thread with a few half-hitch knots (Basics), but do not trim.

[5] Attach a needle to the tail, and exit an 8º opposite the ring of 8ºs added in step 4. Place the focal stone face up in the bezel.

[6] Pick up two 15ºs, an 11º, and two 15ºs, and sew through the 8º again **(figure 4, a–b)**.

[7] Pick up a 15º, and sew through the next 8º **(b–c)**. Pick up two 15ºs and an 11º, and sew through the adjacent two 15ºs in the previous stitch and the 8º your thread just exited **(c–d)**. Repeat these two stitches around. For the last stitch you will only pick up an 11º.

[8] Exit an 11º. Pick up a 15º, and sew through the next 11º **(figure 5, a–b)**. Pick up two 15ºs, and sew through the next 11º **(b–c)**. Repeat these two stitches around, pulling the beadwork snug around the focal stone. Sew through two 15ºs from the previous round to exit near an 8º.

[9] Pick up a 15º, a color A 3mm bicone crystal, and a 15º. Cross the stitch along the edge of the bezel diagonally, and sew through the next two 15ºs, toward the round of 8ºs **(figure 6)**. Repeat around the bezel. End the thread (Basics).

[10] Use the working thread from step 4 to sew through the beadwork, and exit a set of three 11ºs along the edge. Pick up a 15º, an 11º,

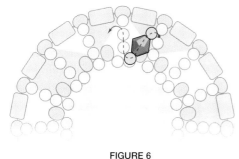

FIGURE 6

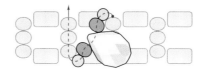

FIGURE 7

EDITOR'S NOTE:
To attach a necklace to the pendant, sew through the 8°s opposite the 15–18mm briolette. String a matching two-strand necklace using a mixture of the beads used to make the bezel.

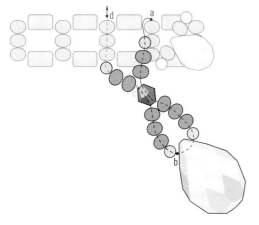

FIGURE 8

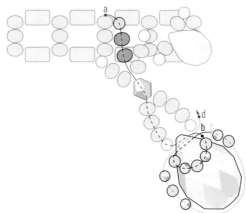

FIGURE 9

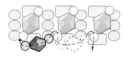

FIGURE 10

a 5–7mm briolette, an 11°, and a 15°, cross the stitch along the edge of the bezel diagonally, and sew through the next three 11°s (figure 7). Repeat twice.

[11] To add the large briolette, pick up a 15°, two 11°s, an A 3mm, three 11°s, a 15°, and a 15–18mm briolette (figure 8, a–b). Pick up a 15° and three 11°s, and sew back through the A 3mm (b–c). Pick up two 11°s and a 15°, cross the stitch diagonally, and sew through the next three 11°s (c–d).

[12] To embellish the briolette, pick up a 15° and two 11°s, and sew down through the A 3mm just added and the next five beads (figure 9, a–b). Pick up a 15°, a 2mm round crystal, a 15°, a 2mm, and a 15°, and sew through the briolette again (b–c). Pick up a 2mm, a 15°, a 2mm, a 15°, and a 2mm, and sew through the briolette again (c–d). Sew through all the beads surrounding the briolette, and sew up through the 15°, three 11°s, and A 3mm. Pick up two 11°s and a 15°, and sew into the remaining corner of the stitch on the bezel.

[13] Sew through the beadwork to exit the next set of three 11°s, so you are positioned as in step 10, and repeat step 10.

[14] Pick up a 15°, a 4mm bicone crystal, and a 15°, cross the stitch diagonally, and sew through the next set of three 11°s. Repeat around the bezel until you reach the briolettes added in step 10.

[15] Exit a 15° added in step 10, pointing toward the front of the pendant. Pick up a 15°, an A 3mm, and a 15°, and sew through the next front 15° from step 10, back to front (figure 10). Repeat around the front of the pendant, alternating A and B 3mms. End the thread.

EDITOR'S NOTES:
• Whether you use a flat-back chessboard cabochon or a pointed-back crystal stone, tension is the key to a nice fitting bezel. Bead the first strip of right-angle weave tightly, and check the fit of the 8°s around the bezel as you stitch the second round. Julie added 15°s between the 8°s when she sewed through the round in step 4.
• Depending on the type of briolettes you use, you may need to adjust the bead counts to let your dangles and embellishments fit nicely.

A
Metalsmith's
Match

This beaded bracelet
simulates granulation,
the ancient art of fusing
tiny metal spheres into
intricate patterns

designed by **Shelley Nybakke**

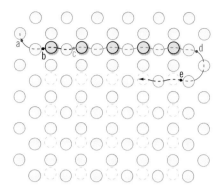

FIGURE 1

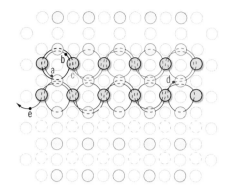

FIGURE 2

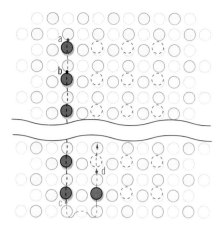

FIGURE 3

MATERIALS

two-tone bangle bracelet
- 50g 11º metal seed beads, color A
- 10g 11º glass or metal seed beads, color B
- Fireline 10 lb. and 6 lb. test
- beading needles, #10

With barely visible threads, the texture of this layered bangle mimics fused gold or silver. Since metal beads are available in many colors, like copper and gunmetal, you can make a monochromatic or multihued bracelet. Or, once you've established the base layer in metal beads, try adding a colorful pattern of glass beads, as in the bangle with the Egyptian-inspired blue-and-gold palette.

stepbystep

Base layer

[1] Center a needle on 4 yd. (3.7m) of 10 lb. Fireline. Working with doubled thread, attach a stop bead (Basics, p. 8), leaving a 6-in. (15cm) tail.

[2] Work in right-angle weave (Right-Angle Weave Basics, p. 5) using color A seed beads to create a row six stitches long.

[3] Continue in right-angle weave until you have a band that is six stitches wide and 70 rows long or the desired length, ending and adding thread (Basics) as needed.

[4] Remove the stop bead, and join the band into a ring by working six stitches of right-angle weave off of the end beads in the first and last rows, using two As for the first stitch and one A for each subsequent stitch.

Second layer

[1] To build a foundation for the second layer, add As to the rows across the width of the base, ending and adding thread as needed: Exit an edge A (figure 1, point a), then sew through the adjacent A (a–b). Pick up an A, and sew through the next A in the row (b–c), pulling the thread tight until the A clicks into place.

Continue to the end of the row (c–d), adding a total of five As. This foundation layer decreases the stitches in the rows of the second layer to five instead of six. Sew through the next two As in the base (d–e).

[2] Repeat step 1 (photo a) until you've added foundation As to each row of the base layer. Sew through the beadwork to exit an A in the foundation layer.

[3] Pick up an A, and sew through an adjacent A in the foundation layer (figure 2, a–b). Pick up an A, and sew through the A your thread exited at the start of this step and the next three As (b–c). Continue working in right-angle weave to finish the row, adding one A per stitch (c–d) and making sure each stitch is snug before adding the next. Repeat (d–e) to complete the second layer.

Third layer

[1] Build a foundation for the third layer lengthwise around the band: Add a doubled length of 6 lb. Fireline to the beadwork, and exit at figure 3, point a. Pick up a color B 11º seed bead, and sew through the next A in the round (a–b), pulling the thread tight until the B clicks into place. Repeat to complete the round (b–c).

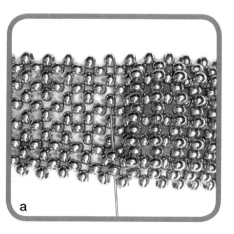

a

b

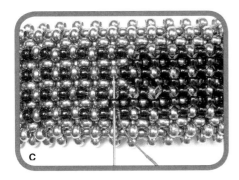

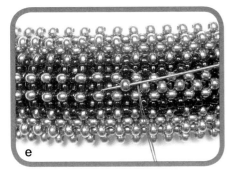

EDITOR'S NOTE:
Smoke-colored Fireline works particularly well with metal beads, because its dark gray color recedes into the beadwork, appearing as a patina rather than as an obtrusive white thread.

[2] Sew through the beadwork to exit an A in the adjacent round. Add a B as in step 2 (c–d), and repeat to complete the round. Add a total of four B foundation rounds (photo b), decreasing the stitches in the rows of the third layer to three instead of five.

[3] Work as in step 3 of the second layer (photo c) to complete the third layer, using Bs instead of As.

Fourth layer

[1] To build a foundation for the fourth layer, add As to the rows across the width of the third layer: Add a doubled length of 6 lb. Fireline to the beadwork, and exit a B added in step 3 of the third layer. Pick up an A, and sew through the next B in the row, pulling tightly until the A clicks into place. Repeat to complete the row. Repeat around, decreasing the stitches in the fourth layer to two instead of three (photo d).

[2] Sew through the beadwork to exit an A in the foundation layer. Work as in step 3 of the second layer, using Bs along the edges and As in the center of the stitches (photo e). Repeat to complete the fourth layer, and end the thread.

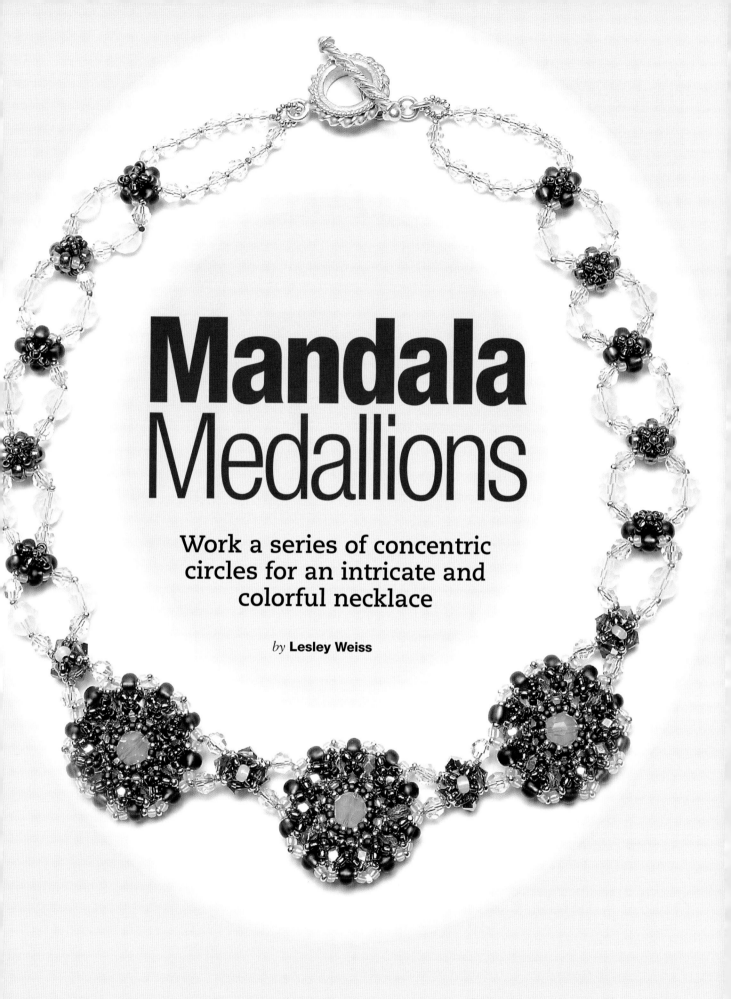

Mandala
Medallions

Work a series of concentric circles for an intricate and colorful necklace

by **Lesley Weiss**

What does angular right-angle weave have in common with the circular art of mandalas? Geometry, of course! Mandalas — circular patterns that work outward from a center — are an ancient tradition featured in several different cultures, religions, and philosophies. As Lesley contemplated the possibilities of circular right-angle weave, the mandala-like pattern of these medallions arose naturally from the geometry of the stitch.

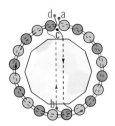

FIGURE 1

stepbystep

Medallions

[1] On 2 yd. (1.8m) of thread, pick up a 13º Charlotte and a 15º seed bead. Repeat until you have 20 beads. Leaving a 6-in. (15cm) tail, sew through the first 10 beads again, and pull to form a snug ring (figure 1, a–b).

[2] Pick up a 6mm round crystal, skip the next nine beads in the ring, and sew through the 10th bead (b–c). Sew back through the crystal, then sew through the bead your thread exited in the same direction. Continue through the next 10 beads in the ring, exiting a 15º (c–d).

[3] Pick up a color A 11º seed bead, a color C 11º seed bead, and an A 11º. Sew through the 15º your thread exited and the first A 11º (figure 2, a–b). Pick up a C 11º and an A 11º, and sew through the next 15º in the base ring. Sew through the A 11º in the previous stitch, the two beads in the new stitch, and the next 15º in the ring (b–c). Continue around the ring, working seven more right-angle weave stitches (Right-Angle Weave Basics, p. 5), sewing through the 15ºs in the ring and skipping the Charlottes (c–d).

[4] To close the ring, pick up a C 11º, and sew through the next A 11º and 15º in the ring. Continue through the previous A 11º and the new C 11º (d–e).

[5] Pick up a Charlotte, a 4mm fire-polished bead, a Charlotte, a color A 6º seed bead, a Charlotte, a 4mm, and a Charlotte. Sew through the C 11º your thread exited at the start of this step, and continue through the first Charlotte and 4mm (e–f).

[6] Pick up a Charlotte, an A 6º, a Charlotte, a 4mm, and a Charlotte, and sew through the next C 11º. Pick up a Charlotte, and sew through the next 4mm and the first four beads just picked up (f–g). Pick up a Charlotte, and sew through the next C 11º. Continue around the ring in modified right-angle weave, and exit the last Charlotte (g–h).

[7] Pick up a C 11º, a Charlotte, and a C 11º, and sew through the next Charlotte, A 6º, and Charlotte (h–i). Repeat around, and end by sewing down through the 4mm adjacent to the last stitch (i–j).

[8] Pick up a Charlotte, a 15º, a color B 11º, an A 11º, and a Charlotte, and sew through the 4mm and the first three beads just picked up (figure 3, a–b). Pick up an A 11º and a Charlotte, and sew

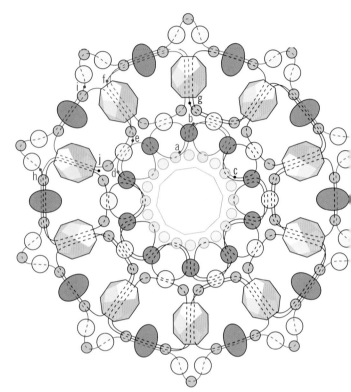

FIGURE 2

FIGURE 3

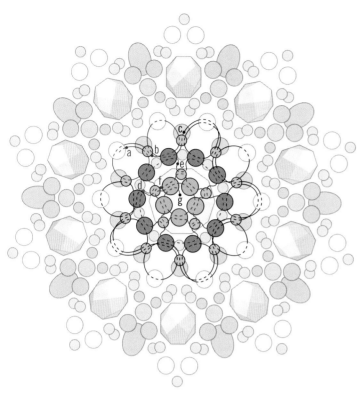

FIGURE 4

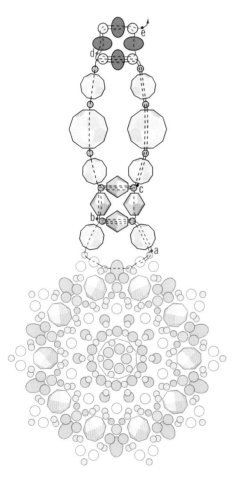

FIGURE 5

down through the next 4mm (b–c). Pick up a Charlotte and a 15º, and sew through the next B 11º, A 11º, Charlotte, and 4mm (c–d). Repeat around the medallion. Weave through the beadwork to exit at **figure 4, point a.**

[9] Flip the beadwork over. Pick up a Charlotte, an A 11º, and a Charlotte, and sew through the C 11º and the first Charlotte again **(a–b)**. Pick up an A 11º and a Charlotte, and sew through the next C 11º and the Charlotte, A 11º, and Charlotte **(b–c)**. Continue around the ring in right-angle weave, exiting the last A 11º added in this round **(c–d)**.

[10] Pick up a Charlotte, and sew through the next two A 11ºs **(d–e)**. Repeat around the ring, and step up through the first Charlotte picked up in this step **(e–f)**.

[11] Pick up a B 11º, and sew through the next Charlotte. Repeat around the ring, and sew through the five B 11ºs again **(f–g)**. End the working thread and tail (Basics, p. 8).

[12] Repeat steps 1–11 to make two more medallions.

Assembly

[1] Add a comfortable length of thread (Basics) in a medallion, and exit a Charlotte on the outer edge (**figure 5, point a**). Pick up a 4mm round crystal, a Charlotte, a 4mm bicone crystal, a Charlotte, and a 4mm round, and sew through the next edge Charlotte, C 11º, Charlotte, A 6º, Charlotte, C 11º, Charlotte, and the first four beads picked up in this step **(a–b)**.

[2] Pick up a 4mm bicone, a Charlotte, a 4mm bicone, a Charlotte, and a 4mm bicone. Sew through the Charlotte, 4mm bicone, and Charlotte that your thread

exited at the start of this step and the next four beads **(b–c)**.

[3] Pick up a 4mm round, a Charlotte, a 6mm round, a Charlotte, a 4mm round, a Charlotte, a C 11º, an A 6º, a C 11º, a Charlotte, a 4mm round, a Charlotte, a 6mm round, a Charlotte, and a 4mm round. Sew through the Charlotte, 4mm bicone, and Charlotte your thread exited at the start of this step and the next nine beads **(c–d)**.

[4] Pick up an A 6º, a C 11º, an A 6º, a C 11º, and an A 6º, and sew through C 11º, A 6º, and C 11º your thread exited at the start of this step and the first four beads picked up in this step **(d–e)**.

[5] Repeat steps 3 and 4 four times, alternating A 6ºs and color B 6º seed beads.

[6] Pick up 12 beads in an alternating pattern of a Charlotte and a 4mm round. Pick up 11 Charlottes and half of the clasp and sew through the last 10 Charlottes again to form a ring (**figure 6, a–b**). Sew through the next two Charlottes of the ring once

MATERIALS
necklace 16½ in. (41.9cm)

- crystals
  23 6mm round
  76 4mm round
  16 4mm bicone
- **30** 4mm fire-polished beads
- seed beads
  5g 6º, color A
  1g 6º, color B
  1g 8º, color C
  4g 11º, in each of **3** colors: A, B, C
  4g 13º Charlotte
  3g 15º
- clasp
- nylon beading thread, size D
- beading needles, #13

The stitches that pull the medallions into shape also create a decorative pattern on the back.

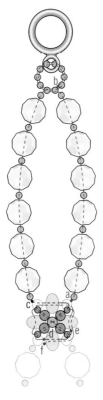

FIGURE 6

more, pick up 12 beads in an alternating pattern of a Charlotte and a 4mm round, and pick up a Charlotte **(b–c)**.
[7] Sew through the next C 11º and 6º. Pick up a 15º, an A 11º, a B 11º, an A 11º, and a 15º, and sew through the 6º opposite the one your thread exited **(c–d)**. Pick up a 15º and an A 11º, sew through the B 11º, pick up an A 11º and a 15º, and sew through the 6º your thread exited at the start of this step and the next C 11º and 6º **(d–e)**. Sew through the 15º, A 11º, B 11º, A 11º, 15º, and

the 6º opposite. Sew through the beads across the stitch in the opposite direction, and sew through the next 6º, C 11º, and 6º **(e–f)**. Flip the necklace over and repeat this step on the opposite side of the cluster.
[8] Sew back through the chain to the next cluster of 6ºs, and repeat step 7. Repeat with the remaining clusters of 6ºs, ending and adding thread (Basics) as needed. For the 4mm bicone cluster, substitute Charlottes for the 15ºs and a color C 8º seed bead for the B 11º. Sew back into the medallion, and end the thread.

[9] Repeat steps 1–8 with a second medallion. Add a new thread in one of the medallions with an attached chain.
[10] Sew through the beadwork to exit the third outer-edge Charlotte from the chain. Repeat steps 1 and 2. Pick up a Charlotte and a 4mm round, and sew through an edge Charlotte on the unattached medallion. Sew through the next C 11º, Charlotte, A 6º, Charlotte, C 11º, and Charlotte. Pick up a 4mm round and a Charlotte, and sew through the next 4mm bicone, Charlotte, and

4mm bicone. Repeat step 7 using the Charlottes and C 8ºs.
[11] Sew through the second medallion to exit the third outer-edge Charlotte from the chain. Repeat step 10 to join the third medallion, sewing into the medallion three outer-edge Charlottes from the second chain. End the threads.

Totally
Twisted

Add variety to your beading repertoire with this spiraling adaptation of right-angle weave

by **Julia Gerlach**

A tube worked with 8º and 11º seed beads is the foundation for this necklace, which you can make long or short. The addition of 3mm beads and more 11ºs accentuates the spiral.

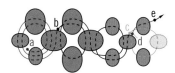

FIGURE 1

stepbystep

Short necklace, p. 75 and far right

Right-angle weave base
[1] On a comfortable length of thread, pick up a color A 11º seed bead, two 8º seed beads, and an A, leaving an 8-in. (20cm) tail. Sew through all four beads again to form a ring, and continue through the first two beads **(figure 1, a–b)**.
[2] Working in right-angle weave (Right-Angle Weave Basics, p. 5), work a stitch with three 8ºs and a stitch with three As **(b–c)**.
[3] To form the right-angle weave strip into a ring, pick up an A, sew through the end A of the first stitch, pick up an A, and sew through the end A of the third stitch **(c–d)**. Continue through the next A **(d–e)**.
[4] For the next round, work the first stitch in tubular right-angle weave (Right-Angle Weave Basics) with two 8ºs and an A **(figure 2, a–b)**. Work the second stitch with two 8ºs **(b–c)**, the third stitch with two As **(c–d)**, and the final stitch with an A **(d–e)**.
[5] Repeat step 4 until the rope is half the desired length of the necklace, ending and adding thread (Basics, p. 8) as needed.
[6] Make a second rope the same length, but alter the pattern so that it spirals in the opposite direction:
Base round: Pick up two 8ºs and two As, and form a ring

(figure 3, a–b). Work the second stitch with three 8ºs **(b–c)**, the third stitch with two As and an 8º **(c–d)**, and the fourth stitch (forming the ring) with two As **(d–e)**.
Round 2: Work the first stitch with an A and two 8ºs **(figure 4, a–b)**, the second stitch with two As **(b–c)**, the third stitch with an 8º and an A **(c–d)**, and the fourth stitch with an 8º **(d–e)**.
Round 3: Work the first stitch with an 8º and two As **(figure 5, a–b)**, the second stitch with two 8ºs **(b–c)**, the third stitch with an A and an 8º **(c–d)**, and the fourth stitch with an A **(d–e)**.
[7] Repeat rounds 2 and 3 until the second rope is the same length as the first. End the working thread and tail.

Embellishment
[1] Add a comfortable length of thread at one end of one of the ropes, and exit an end 8º.
[2] Pick up a color B 11º seed bead, and sew through the next 8º in the round **(figure 6, a–b)**. Pick up a B, cross diagonally over the opening in the middle of the stitch, and sew through the 8º on the opposite side of the stitch **(b–c)**.
[3] Sew through the next 8º in the stitch you just crossed over, and pick up a color C 11º. Sew through the next two 8ºs in the stitch, pick up a C, and sew through the 8º your thread exited at the start of this step **(figure 7)**.

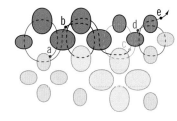

FIGURE 2

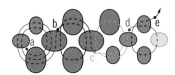

FIGURE 3

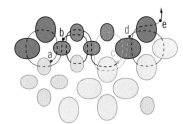

FIGURE 4

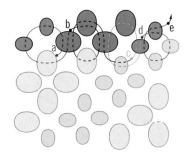

FIGURE 5

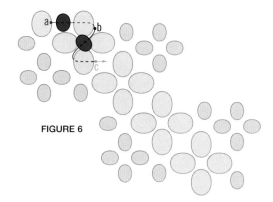

FIGURE 6

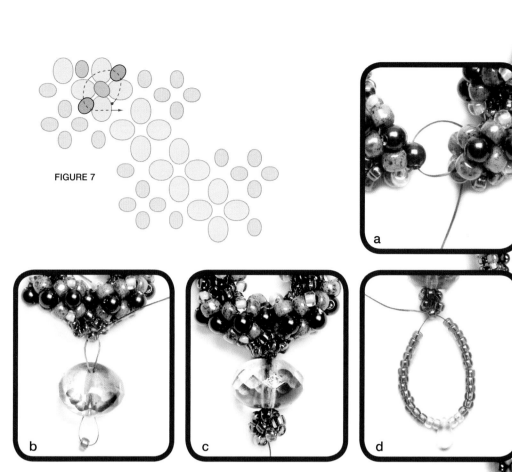

FIGURE 7

a

b

c

d

[4] Repeat steps 2 and 3 for approximately 3 in. (7.6cm), ending and adding thread as needed.

[5] For the rest of the rope, continue embellishing as in steps 2 and 3, but substitute 3mm beads for the Bs. This will make one end of the rope thicker than the other.

[6] Repeat steps 1–5 to embellish the other rope. Before you reach the end, align the ropes so they come together in a point. Instead of adding the last 3mm, sew through the end 3mm of the other rope **(photo a)**. Sew the ends together where they join. Always sew through the beads, not around them, and follow the right-angle weave thread path as needed.

Looped fringe

[1] Exiting a bead where the two ropes join, pick up a 7 x 11mm accent bead.

[2] Pick up an A, and sew back through the accent bead and the bead your thread exited at the start of step 1 **(photo b)**. Sew through an adjacent bead, and sew through the accent bead again. Snug up the accent bead to the necklace.

[3] Repeat step 2 three times to connect the accent bead evenly at the end of the necklace and to add four As below the accent bead.

[4] Sew through one of the As added below the accent bead, and, using As, work a round of tubular right-angle weave stitches using the four beads as the base **(photo c)**.

[5] Exit an end bead of the group of right-angle weave stitches you just made. Pick up 10 As, three Bs, two Cs, a drop bead, two Cs, three Bs, and 10 As. Sew through the bead your thread just exited to make a loop **(photo d)**.

[6] Sew through the next end bead, and repeat step 5. Continue making one loop off of each bead in the last round for a total of 12 loops. When you make the loops on the side and top beads of each stitch, pick up fewer As (seven or eight) so that those loops are slightly shorter than the ones on the very end. End the working thread.

[7] Thread a needle on the tail at one end of the necklace. Pick up seven 15º seed beads and one half of the clasp, and sew through the bead in the end round that is opposite the one your thread is exiting **(photo e)**. Pick up two 15ºs, and sew through the middle three 15ºs of the seven previously picked up **(photo f)**. Pick up two 15ºs, and sew through the end bead your thread exited at the start of this step. Retrace the thread path several times, and end the tail.

[8] Repeat step 7 on the other end of the necklace.

Accent beads and fringe loops finish the ends of this long necklace.

Long necklace, above

[1] Follow steps 1–5 of "Right-angle weave base," but stitch the rope to the desired necklace length.

[2] Beginning at one end of the rope, embellish as in "Embellishment," but begin with 3mms instead of Bs. Continue with this substitution for approximately one-third the length of the rope. Switch to Bs instead of 3mms for the next one-third, and go back to 3mms for the final third. End the working thread and tail.

[3] Add a comfortable length of thread at one end of the rope, and exit an end bead. Add fringe loops as in steps 5 and 6 of "Looped fringe," and end the working thread and tail.

[4] Add a comfortable length of thread at the other end. Repeat steps 2–4 of "Looped fringe" twice to add two accent beads, and then add fringe loops as you did at the other end of the rope. End the working threads.

MATERIALS

both necklaces
- nylon beading thread, size D, or Fireline 6 lb. test
- beading needles, #11

short necklace with clasp 18 in. (46cm)
- 7 x 11mm faceted glass accent bead
- 12 4 x 6mm drop beads
- 16-in. (41cm) strand 3mm round Swarovski pearls
- seed beads
  15g 8º
  10g 11º, color A
  5g 11º in each of **2** colors: B, C
  22 15º
- clasp

long necklace without clasp 32 in. (81cm)
- 2 11 x 17mm faceted glass accent beads
- 24–32 4 x 6mm drop beads
- 2 16-in. (41cm) strands 3mm faceted gemstone beads
- seed beads
  30g 8º
  20g 11º, color A
  10g 11º in each of **2** colors: B, C

Broad Band

Communicate your style loud and clear with metallic seed beads and crystals

designed by **Barbara Klann**

Cubic right-angle weave produces a tube of dimensional beadwork in the form of a substantial yet flexible band with holes that beg to be filled with the flash of crystals.

stepbystep

Base

[1] On a comfortable length of thread, pick up four color A 8º seed beads, and tie them into a ring with a square knot (Basics, p. 8), leaving a 6-in. (15cm) tail. Sew through the next two As in the ring.

[2] Working in cubic right-angle weave, (Right-Angle Weave Basics, p. 5), stitch the four walls of a cube with As. Sew through the beads of the open end to cinch them closed (photo a).

[3] Continue in cubic right-angle weave, ending and adding thread (Basics) as needed, until you reach the desired length, leaving 1¼ in. (3.2cm) for the clasp.

[4] Work a second row of cubic right-angle weave off of the first using color B 8º seed beads: The edge of the first row consists of groups of four As, which will serve as the rings that the new row will be built off of. To start the first stitch in the new row, pick up three Bs, and sew through the A your thread exited at the start of this step and the next A in the ring (photo b).

[5] Continue in cubic right-angle weave using Bs until you reach the end of the row (photo c).

[6] Work a third row using As. End the working thread and tail.

[7] Add thread, exiting an end A on the other edge of the first row of cubic right-angle weave. Repeat steps 4–6 on this side of the bracelet.

[8] Add thread to one end of the band, exiting an A in the center row. Pick up a B, sew through the opposite A in the end stitch, back through the B, and through the A your thread exited at the start of this step. Working in ladder stitch (Basics), attach two Bs to the first B. Set the band aside.

Clasp
Toggle ring

[1] On a comfortable length of thread, center 40 15º seed beads. Sew through the first 15º again, forming a ring (figure 1, a–b).

[2] Work two rounds of circular peyote (Basics) off the first using 15ºs (b–c). Work two rounds using 11º cylinder beads (c–d). Work one round using 11º seed beads (d–e).

[3] Using the tail, work two rounds using cylinders, then zip up (Basics) the two end rounds. (The end rounds don't seem to line up properly, but as you zip them up, the beadwork twists to accommodate the gap.)

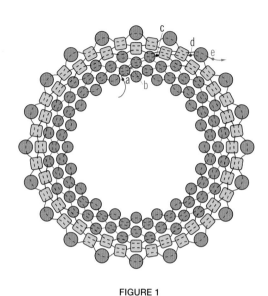

FIGURE 1

FIGURE 2

MATERIALS
bracelet 8½ in. (21.6cm)
- **2** 4mm bicone crystals
- **43** 3.2mm crystal montees or 2mm round crystals
- 25g 8º seed beads in each of **2** colors: A, B
- 1–2g 11º seed beads
- 1g 11º cylinder beads
- 1–2g 15º seed beads
- nylon beading thread
- beading needles, #12

EDITOR'S NOTE:
Working only one row of Bs on each side of the first row will result in a thinner band.

[4] Exit an 11º along the outer edge, and pick up a B. Sew through the next 11º in the round **(photo d)**. Retrace the thread path along the outer edge so that you can make a second thread pass through the B. End the working thread and tail, and set the ring aside.

Toggle bar
[1] On a comfortable length of thread, center 12 11ºs, and work 12 rows of even-count peyote (Basics).
[2] Zip up the end rows to form a tube.
[3] Sew through the center of the tube, exiting one end. Pick up a 4mm bicone crystal and a 15º. Sew back through the 4mm and out the other end of the tube. Repeat to add a second 4mm. Retrace the thread path several times, and end the working thread.

[4] Using the tail, sew through the first 11º in a row. Pick up a 15º, and sew through the next 11º in the same row. Repeat to add a 15º between each pair of 11ºs in the row, then repeat to complete the embellishment on the remaining rows.
[5] Sew through the beadwork to exit a 15º at the center of the tube. Pick up a B, and sew through the next 15º in the same row **(photo e)**. End the tail.

Assembly
[1] Using the working thread exiting the ladder at the end of the band, sew through the B on the toggle bar and the last B in the ladder **(photo f)**. Retrace the thread path several times to secure the join, then exit the end A in the first row of cubic right-angle weave **(figure 2, point a).**

[2] Pick up a montee or 2mm round, and sew through the opposite A **(a–b)**. Sew back through the crystal and the opposite A **(b–c)**. Sew through the next two As **(c–d)**. Repeat to add a crystal embellishment to the center of each stitch in the row of As.
[3] Exiting the end A in the row, pick up a B, and work one ladder stitch. Sew through the B on the toggle ring **(photo g)**, and reinforce the join. End

Link_{by}Link

A chain of interlocking beaded links forms a flexible bracelet

designed by **Hannah Benninger**

A beaded cube is the building block for these three-dimensional rectangle- and square-shaped links.

stepbystep

Links

[1] On 1 yd. (.9m) of thread, pick up four color A 15º seed beads, leaving a 6-in. (15cm) tail. Sew through the As again to form a ring, and continue through the next A.

[2] Working in cubic right-angle weave (Right-Angle Weave Basics, p. 5), stitch the four walls of a cube using A 15ºs. Sew through the beads of the open end to cinch them closed.

[3] Work in cubic right-angle weave to stitch a total of six joined cubes.

[4] With the thread exiting the bottom A on one edge of the end cube, work three more cubes to form your beadwork into the shape of an L. You have now established the inside and outside edges of the link.

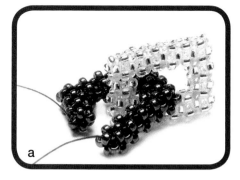
a

b

c

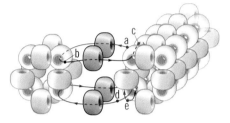
FIGURE 1

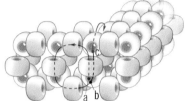
FIGURE 2

[5] With the thread exiting the bottom A on the inside edge of the end cube, work five more cubes.

[6] With the thread exiting the bottom A on the inside edge of the end cube, work one cube.

[7] To connect the first and last cubes, pick up an A, and sew through the opposite A of the first cube (figure 1, a–b). Pick up an A, and sew through the A the thread exited at the start of this step (b–c). Snug up the beads. Sew through the next two edge As (c–d). Repeat to add two more As (d–e).

[8] On one side of the connection, sew through the four As that are not connected in a ring (figure 2, a–b). Sew through the first A again (b–c). Sew through the opposite side of the cube, and repeat to close the other open side. End the working thread and tail (Basics, p. 8).

[9] Repeat steps 1–8 to make a total of nine color A links.

[10] Work as in steps 1–9 to make a color B link that is five by five cubes square. Before completing the link, slide it through a color A link (photo a). Complete the color B link as in steps 8 and 9.

[11] Make eight more color B links as in step 10, but before completing each of the remaining color B links, slide it through the previously attached color A link, and attach another color A link (photo b). Complete the color B link.

[12] Add or omit pairs of color A and B links to lengthen or shorten the bracelet.

Toggle bar

[1] On 1½ yd. (1.4m) of thread, make a color B link, and connect it to the end color A link. Sew through the beadwork to exit an edge B of the third cube on any side of the link.

[2] Work four cubes, then work two cubes on each side of the end cube to complete the toggle bar. End the threads (photo c).

EDITOR'S NOTE:
If this is your first attempt at cubic right-angle weave, it will be easier to practice the stitch using 11° or 8° seed beads. Once you become familiar with how the beads form the cube, switch to 15°s to make the project.

MATERIALS
bracelet 7½ in. (19.1cm)
- 6g 15° seed beads in each of 2 colors: A, B
- nylon beading thread, colors to match color A and B seed beads
- beading needles, #13

Four Square

A repeating motif gives this necklace a modern edge

designed by **Cathy Lampole**

Mirrored increases and decreases in right-angle weave create square-shaped embellishments on a flexible rope. A pendant made of square crystal rings echoes the pattern.

stepbystep

Rope

[1] On 2 yd. (1.8m) of color A thread, pick up four color A 11º seed beads, leaving a 6-in. (15cm) tail. Sew through the first three beads again to form a ring (figure 1, a–b). Picking up three As per stitch, work two right-angle weave stitches (Right-Angle Weave Basics, p. 5 and b–c).

[2] Pick up an A. Fold the strip in half, aligning the ends, and sew through the end A of the first stitch (figure 2, a–b). Pick up an A. Sew through the end A of the third stitch and the next three beads of the new stitch (b–c).

[3] Work in tubular right-angle weave (Right-Angle Weave Basics) until the rope is the desired length, ending and adding thread (Basics, p. 8) as needed. Sew through a few more beads of the tube to secure the thread. Do not end the working thread or tail.

Square embellishments

[1] Add a comfortable length of color B thread at one end of the rope. Exit an A three beads from the end.

FIGURE 1

FIGURE 2

FIGURE 3

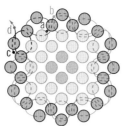

FIGURE 4

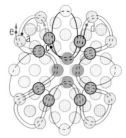

FIGURE 5

MATERIALS

necklace 19½ in. (49.5cm)
with pendant 3¾ in.
(9.5cm)

• **4** 20mm Swarovski
  square rings (#4439)
• **30** 4mm bicone crystals
• 11º seed beads
  25g color A (rope base
  color)
  35g color B (embellish-
  ment color)
• nylon beading thread,
  size B, to match each
  seed bead color
• beading needles, #13

a

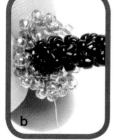

b

c

d

e

f

g

[2] Pick up three color B 11º seed beads. Sew through the A in the rope and the first B added **(figure 3, a–b)**.

[3] To begin an increase, pick up three Bs. Sew through the B your thread exited in the previous stitch, the three Bs just picked up, and the next A in the rope **(b–c)**. You'll complete the increase in the next round.

[4] Pick up two Bs. Sew through the last B picked up in the previous stitch, the A your thread just exited in the rope, and the first B just picked up **(c–d)**.

[5] Repeat steps 3 **(d–e)** and 4 **(e–f)** twice **(f–g)**.

[6] Pick up two Bs, and work the last stitch to complete the first round of the first square **(g–h** and **photo a)**. Because of the increases you began at the corners, you now have 12

edge beads (three on each side) in round 1.

[7] To stitch round 2, work 12 right-angle weave stitches using Bs. Work one stitch off of each edge bead: Pick up three Bs in the first stitch **(figure 4, a–b)**, two Bs in each of the next 10 stitches **(b–c)**, and one B in the last stitch **(c–d)**. Round 2 has 12 edge beads and curves away from round 1 **(photo b)**.

[8] Round 3 brings the beadwork back in toward the rope and connects to it. To begin, make sure your thread is exiting a B at the end of one side **(point d)**. Work a decrease by sewing through the next edge B in round 2 **(figure 5, a–b)**. This should be the end B on the next side. Pick up two Bs, and sew through the two Bs in round 2 your thread just exited and

the first new B **(b–c)**. Sew through the next A in the rope that is parallel to the one from which you began the square embellishment **(photo c)**. Pick up a B, and sew through the next edge B in the previous round, the adjacent B in the previous stitch, the A in the rope that your thread just exited **(photo d)**, and the B just picked up **(c–d)**. Repeat around, adding a total of eight beads in this round **(d–e)**.

[9] Sew through the rope to exit an A four beads away from where the embellishment ended **(photo e)**. Repeat steps 2–8 to stitch a second square. The beads in the rope between the squares form an X **(photo f)**.

[10] Continue, adding an even number of squares along the length of the rope.

Add or remove rounds of the rope as needed to accommodate the number of squares. Leave the last five rounds of the rope unembellished. End the working thread.

Clasp

[1] Add 1 yd. (.9m) of color A thread at the end of the rope where you began making the square embellishments, and exit an end A. Using As and working off two adjacent end beads in the rope, work a flat right-angle weave strip that is two stitches wide and long enough to encircle one side of a crystal square (about seven stitches long) **(photo g)**.

[2] Slide the strip through a crystal square, and stitch the end of the strip to the other two end beads of the rope

85

h

i

j

k

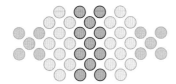

FIGURE 6

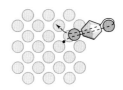

FIGURE 7

(photo h). Retrace the thread path to reinforce the join, and end the working thread.

[3] To make a toggle bar, work a right-angle weave tube that is four stitches around and seven stitches long. Sew through the four beads at each end to cinch the tube closed. Sew through the toggle bar, and exit a bead in the center stitch. Sew the remaining end of the rope to the center stitch of the toggle bar (photo i). Retrace the thread path to reinforce the join, and end the working thread.

Pendant

[1] Identify the two center square embellishments, and add 2 yd. (1.8m) of color B thread in one of them. Working toward the center of the necklace, stitch a round of right-angle weave all the way around the square. Work another round to connect the previous round to the next square embellishment (figure 6 and photo j).

[2] Working off the front bottom edge of the large center embellishment, stitch a strip of right-angle weave

that is two stitches wide and six stitches long. Slide the strip through a crystal square. Stitch the end of the strip to the bottom edge at the back of the large center embellishment. Do not end the thread.

[3] On 1 yd. (.9m) of color B thread, stitch a strip of right-angle weave that is three stitches wide and 13 stitches long. Do not end the working thread.

[4] Connect a second crystal square to the first with the strip from the previous step. Sew the ends of the strip together to form a ring.

[5] Adjust the ring so that the thread is exiting between the crystal squares and there is an edge bead directly opposite the bead your thread is exiting. Stitch the edge beads of the strip together between the crystal squares with one right-angle weave stitch (photo k). This will hold the crystal squares in place. Sew through the beadwork to the opposite side of the ring, and repeat.

[6] Repeat steps 3–5 to connect the last crystal square.

[7] To embellish the pendant with crystals, sew through the strip, and exit a B where you want to add a crystal. Pick up a B, a 4mm bicone crystal, and a B. Skip the second B, sew back through the 4mm and the first B, and continue through an adjacent B in the strip (figure 7). Repeat as desired on the strips connecting the crystal squares and the large center embellishment. End the working threads and tails.

EDITOR'S NOTE:
Slide the first round of the rope and the toggle onto a coffee stirrer or small straw. Stitch the tube around the stirrer until the rope is long enough to hold. Besides giving you something to hold onto, the stirrer will also keep the stitches in place so they don't collapse into the center of the tube.